Schöningh

EinFach
Englisch
Unterrichtsmodell

"Strange Fruit" and Other Songs

Cries for Social Consciousness and Civil Rights

Edited by
Iris Edelbrock

Series Editor:
Hans Kröger

Einzelarbeit
Partnerarbeit
Gruppenarbeit
Unterrichtsgespräch
Schreibauftrag
Hausaufgabe
Audio-CD
filmische Präsentation
Projekt, offene Aufgabe
kreative Aufgabe
szenisches Spiel, Rollenspiel

Vorwort

Der Titel der Reihe **EinFach Englisch** verdeutlicht Zielsetzung und Programm zugleich. Einerseits soll Schülerinnen und Schülern auf einfache Art und Weise der Zugang zu klassischen, aber auch neuen literarischen Werken und Filmen ermöglicht werden, andererseits sollen Lehrerinnen und Lehrern in der Praxis erprobte Unterrichtsmodelle angeboten werden, die die wichtigsten methodisch-didaktischen Ansätze ihres Faches Englisch abdecken. Dabei sind die Modelle direkt, ohne langes Einlesen einsetzbar und stellen Unterrichtsarbeit konkret vor. Als besonders hilfreich für die Praxis haben sich dabei folgende Aspekte erwiesen, die für die Gestaltung der Reihe wesentlich sind:

- Überblick über **Figurenkonstellation**, ggf. **Filmszenen** und **Inhalt**
- **Klausuren** mit **Erwartungshorizont**
- **Arbeitsblätter, Tafelbilder** und **Leitfragen** für den Unterricht
- **Piktogramme** als Hinweise auf **Unterrichts-** und **Arbeitsformen**

Das Prinzip der „**Components**" ermöglicht darüber hinaus den variablen Einsatz der Modelle in unterschiedlich konzipierten Unterrichtsreihen. Dabei stehen Machbarkeit und Praxisnähe stets im Vordergrund.

Sprachliche Betreuung: Simone Duxbury-Ziemer

www.schoeningh-schulbuch.de
Schöningh Verlag, Jühenplatz 1–3, 33098 Paderborn

Druck 5 4 3 2 1 / Jahr 2013 12 11 10 09
Die letzte Zahl bezeichnet das Jahr dieses Druckes.

Umschlaggestaltung: Jennifer Kirchhof
Druck und Bindung: AZ Druck und Datentechnik GmbH, Kempten (Allgäu)

ISBN 978-3-14-041246-9

Getting started

The lynching of Lige Daniels, August 3, 1920

Mississippi state sign

Magnolia

Soft summer breeze
Makes me think of my baby
I left down in New Orleans
I left down in New Orleans
Magnolia, you sweet thing
You're driving me mad
Got to get back to you, babe
You're the best I ever had
You're the best I ever had
You whisper "good morning"
So gently in my ear
I'm coming home to you, babe
I'll soon be there
I'll soon be there

"Magnolia", 1972, M+T: J. J. Cale, © by Johnny Bienstock Music/ Artemis Muziekuitgeverij B.V.; SVL: Neue Welt Musikverlag GmbH & Co KG

A blossoming Magnolia tree

- What do you associate with Magnolia trees? What does the Mississippi state sign suggest to the visitor?
- Describe the situation in the picture showing the lynching. Imagine the people's thoughts. What might have been the reason for the lynching and where do you think it has taken place?

Strange Fruit and Other Songs

Component 2: Fortsetzung

Component 3: Political protest songs in the tradition of the Civil Rights Movement **48**

Der Inhalt

Das Musikstück ***Strange Fruit*** **(*Copy 1*, S. 18)** erlangte vor allem durch die von Billie Holiday im Jahre 1939 gesungene Version Weltruhm. Nachdem sie das von Abel Meeropol (Pseudonym Lewis Allen) getextete und komponierte Lied zunächst im New Yorker Nightclub Café Society vorgetragen hatte, erlangte es sehr schnell Bekanntheit über New York und die USA hinaus. Das *TIME Magazine* kürte den Song 1999 zu *dem* Song des 20. Jahrhunderts.
Es wird als eine der ausdrucksstärksten künstlerischen Aussagen gegen die Lynchmorde, vor allem im Süden der USA, angesehen und wurde damit zu einem frühen musikalischen Ausdruck der amerikanischen Bürgerrechtsbewegung und Vorläufer weiterer Protestsongs. Seit seiner Entstehung im Jahre 1937 haben zahlreiche Interpreten das Lied gespielt und gesungen – es hat von seiner Ausdruckskraft bis heute nichts verloren.

In alternierender Reihenfolge beschreiben die Verse die Schönheit und die hochherrschaftliche Eleganz der amerikanischen Südstaaten, den betörenden Duft der Magnolien und kontrastieren sie in drastischer Weise mit der brutalen und ekelerregenden Realität der Lynchmorde und dem Leiden der gequälten Menschen. Der Schönheit und Fruchtbarkeit des amerikanischen Südens, hier symbolisiert durch die Magnolie (die auch Symbol des Staates Mississippi ist), wird geradezu ein Schlachthofszenario aus Blut und vom Schmerz verzerrten Gesichtern gegenübergestellt. Das Bild der Frucht fortführend, geht die dritte Strophe (indirekt) auf die Ernte ein: die Frucht ist „bitter", sozusagen ungenießbar, sie verrottet in der Sonne, ist gefundenes Fressen für die Krähen (→ Aasfresser; oft auch Symbol des Todesboten in der Mythologie).
Im formalen Aufbau ist das Lied eher unauffällig: Es besteht aus drei Strophen mit je vier Zeilen und einem durchgängigen Paarreim. Die eigentliche Dynamik und Aussagekraft entsteht durch die (meist kontrastiv eingesetzten) Verben und Adjektive.
Vor allem die besondere Vortragsweise Billie Holidays beeindruckte das Publikum, sie wurde als „psychisch verstörend oder gar physisch schmerzhaft" empfunden und auch mit dem Bild „Der Schrei" des expressionistischen Malers Edvard Munch verglichen (s.a. S. 17).
Weitere Informationen zur Geschichte und Wirkung des Liedes finden Sie im Internet unter http://de.wikipedia.org/wiki/Strange_Fruit, en.wikipedia.org/wiki/Strange_Fruit sowie bei YouTube, das einen Live-Mitschnitt eines Billie-Holiday-Vortrags des Liedes bietet: www.youtube.com/watch?v=h4ZyuULy9zs.

Die Geschichte der amerikanischen ***Protest Songs*** reicht bis in das 18. Jahrhundert zurück, jedoch wurde die Tradition dessen, was man heute mit Protestlied verbindet, im 20. Jahrhundert im Zusammenhang mit der Arbeiterbewegung und der *Great Depression* begründet. Die Website http://en.wikipedia.org/wiki/Protest_song bietet hierzu weitreichende Informationen, viele Beispiele und historische sowie politische Bezüge.

Die in diesem Unterrichtsmodell enthaltenen *Protest Songs* **(*Copy 12*, S. 42; *Copy 13*, S. 43; *Copy 16*, S. 51; *Copy 18*, S. 54; *Copy 19*, S. 55)** stammen zu fast gleichen Teilen von weißen wie von afroamerikanischen Interpreten und decken eine Zeitspanne von 1929 bis 1991 ab. Sie sollen einen kleinen Einblick in das Genre gewähren, sind jedoch eng an den thematischen Zusammenhang mit *Strange Fruit, racism, segregation and social consciousness* angelehnt. Seit 9/11 und dem Irak-Krieg erlebt die Tradition des *Protest Songs* in den USA eine regelrechte Renaissance; viele Künstler, von Neil Young, Tom Waits und Bruce Springsteen bis hin zu Pink, Eminem und den Dixie Chicks, haben die Tradition des *Protest Songs* wieder aufgegriffen und in zeitgemäßer Weise interpretiert.

Vorüberlegungen zum Einsatz der Materialien im Unterricht

Der Song ***Strange Fruit*** wurde von einigen Kritikern als „song of the century" bezeichnet. Wenngleich 70 Jahre alt, thematisiert er ein dunkles Kapitel amerikanischer Geschichte, das bis heute nicht an Brisanz verloren hat.
Eine sozialgeschichtliche, politische sowie psychologisch-emotionale Aufarbeitung der Sklaverei, der Rassentrennung und der damit verbundenen Verbrechen, Vorurteile und Grausamkeiten hat in den USA nur oberflächlich stattgefunden. In einem politisch und gesellschaftlich eher konservativ ausgerichteten Land wie den USA haben sich liberale und linksorientierte Künstler und Intellektuelle (fast) immer in der Opposition gesehen und so ist es nicht verwunderlich, dass es eine große Bandbreite politischer und sozialkritischer Protestsongs gibt, die bis in die Anfänge des 19. Jahrhunderts zurückreichen.

Das vorliegende Unterrichtsmodell konzentriert sich im Zusammenhang mit dem Song *Strange Fruit* auf die unmittelbar damit verknüpften Themen *racism, segregation, lynching* sowie *Civil Rights Movement.*
Die begleitende Audio-CD bietet eine kleine Auswahl von Interpretationen des Songs, die Liste der Interpreten ließe sich jedoch (fast) beliebig fortsetzen: sie reicht von Bessie Smith, Pete Seeger, Eartha Kitt und Diana Ross bis zu Cassandra Wilson, Dee Dee Bridgewater, Sting und UB40, um nur einige zu nennen.

In Ergänzung mit weiteren Materialien, wie Kurzgeschichten, Gedichten, Zeitungsartikeln sowie Fotos und Cartoons gewinnen die Schülerinnen und Schüler einen Einblick in die Thematik. Die Literatur- und Materialienliste im Anhang (S. 56f.) bietet weitere Vorschläge für Songs, mit denen man das Thema, je nach Schwerpunktsetzung und zeitlicher Planung, auch an die obligatorischen Unterrichtsthemen *American dream* oder/und *war/violence* anknüpfen und erweitern kann.

Viele der abgebildeten Lynching-Fotos sind dem Band *Without Sanctuary – Lynching Photography in America* entnommen, der neben vielen historischen Bilddokumenten auch zeitgenössische Äußerungen in Briefen, Interviews usw. bereithält und damit eine sehr gute „Fundgrube" für weiteres Unterrichtsmaterial ist. Der Bildband basiert auf der gleichnamigen Ausstellung, die im Jahre 2001 in der New Yorker Roth Horowitz Gallery ihren Anfang nahm, und ist 2007 bei Twin Palms Publishers erschienen.
Eine weitere, hervorragende Quelle für Bildmaterial zum Thema ist der umfangreiche Band *Freedom – A photographic history of the African American struggle,* im Jahre 2002 erschienen bei Phaidon.
Sehr empfehlenswert ist in diesem thematischen Zusammenhang der umfangreiche Bild- und Textband *We shall overcome* von Herb Boyd aus dem Jahr 2004, verlegt bei Sourcebooks. Neben umfassendem Bildmaterial bietet er Songtexte, weitere Dokumente und Karten sowie Auszüge aus Reden und politischen Manifesten. Dem Buch sind zwei Audio-CDs beigefügt, auf denen historische Tondokumente von Bürgerrechtsaktionen, politische Reden und Songtexte zu finden sind.

Klausuren

Im Folgenden werden zwei Klausurvorschläge zu den Themenbereichen *racism/Civil Rights* und *dealing with racism/guilt* vorgestellt. Es handelt sich um unterschiedliche Textsorten, zum einen um einen Songtext von Bob Dylan aus der Ära der Bürgerrechtsbewegung, zum anderen um einen Sachtext, einen politischen Kommentar, veröffentlicht in der *International Herald Tribune* im April 2008.

Klausur 1 präsentiert einen Protestsong von Bob Dylan aus dem Jahr 1963, der als authentisches Dokument der Zeit des *Civil Rights Movement* gesehen werden kann. Der Text ist als sprachlich nicht so anspruchsvoll einzustufen und kann problemlos in einem Grundkurs eingesetzt werden. Die Klausur kann in Zusammenhang mit *Component 2* gestellt werden, z. B. in Verbindung mit dem Bob-Dylan-Song *The death of Emmett Till* sowie dem politisch-geschichtlichen Hintergrund der *segregation* und des *Civil Rights Movement.* Denkbar wäre eine Einbindung der Klausur auch in *Component 3,* da hier der Schwerpunkt auf verschiedenen Protestliedern liegt und somit eine vergleichende Analyse möglich wäre. Vor allem der von Nina Simone 1964 veröffentlichte Song *Mississippi Goddam'* bietet viele Anknüpfungspunkte – ebenso wie der Dylan-Song ist auch dieses Lied eine Reaktion auf die Ermordung Medgar Evers.

Klausur 2 ist sprachlich etwas anspruchsvoller und als insgesamt mittelschwerer Text einzustufen. Die Schülerinnen und Schüler sollten mit der Textsorte „Kommentar" vertraut sein sowie eine Argumentationsstruktur erkennen und (stilistisch) nachweisen können. Auch aufgrund seiner Länge (719 Wörter) eignet der Text sich gut für einen Leistungskurs. Das Verständnis und die Analyse des Textes setzt eine vorherige Auseinandersetzung mit der Thematik *lynching, Jim Crow* sowie der Problematik der (Nicht-)Anerkennung von Schuld in Zusammenhang mit *slavery* und *segregation* voraus, daher sollte diese Klausur erst im Anschluss an die Erarbeitung von *Component 2* gestellt werden. Der Text bietet darüber hinaus Parallelen zur deutschen Geschichte und dem Umgang damit und könnte daher in voller Länge auch als Grundlage für eine *political debate,* also eine Art Rollenspiel im Klassenzimmer genutzt werden. Er bietet viele Ansatzpunkte für eine sehr kontroverse Diskussion.

Bob Dylan: Only a pawn in their game

A bullet from the back of a bush took Medgar Ever's blood.
A finger fired the trigger to his name.
A handle hid out of the dark
A hand set the spark
Two eyes took the aim
Behind a man's brain
But he can't be blamed
He's only a pawn in their game.

A South politician preaches to the poor white man,
"You got more than the blacks, don't complain.
You're better than them, you been born with white skin," they explain.
And the negro's name
Is used it is plain
For the politician's gain
As he rises to fame
And the poor white remains
On the caboose of the train
But it ain't him to blame
He's only a pawn in their game.

The deputy sheriffs, the soldiers, the governors get paid,
And the marshals and cops get the same,
But the poor white man's used in the hands of them like a tool.
He's taught in his school
From the start by the rule
That the laws are with him
To protect his white skin
To keep up his hate
So he never thinks straight
'Bout the shape that he's in
but it ain't him to blame
He's only a pawn in their game.

From the poverty shacks, he looks from the cracks to the tracks,
And the hoof beats pound in his brain.
And he's taught how to walk in a pack
Shoot in the back
With his fist in a clinch
To hang and to lynch
To hide 'neath the hood
To kill with no pain
Like a dog on a chain
He ain't got no name
But it ain't him to blame
He's only a pawn in their game.

trigger the part of the gun that you press in order to fire it
handle here: the part of the gun that you use to hold it

pawn a chess piece of the least value *(Bauer)*

plain simply, only

caboose part at the back of a train where the person who is in charge rides

shape here: condition, situation

shack a small wooden building
cracks narrow space or opening; or here: from a low social position
hoof beats *Hufschläge*
pound *pochen*
to walk in a pack here: to walk behind the leaders
hood reference to the hoods of the KKK dress; (*US sl*) villain

Today, Medgar Evers was buried from the bullet he caught.
They lowered him down as a king.
But when the shadowy sun sets on the one
That fired the gun
You'll see by his grave
On the stone that remains
Carved next to his name
His epitaph plain:
Only a pawn in their game. *(338 words)*

Only a Pawn in Their Game, 1963, Text & Musik: Bob Dylan, © Special Rider Music.

to lower sb down to let the coffin down into the grave on a rope
the sun sets on the one (*fig*) when sb dies

epitaph words written about a dead person on a gravestone

Note: Bob Dylan wrote this song about the assassination of the African American civil rights activist Medgar Evers on June 12, 1963. Evers was murdered by Byron De La Beckwith, a member of the Ku Klux Klan. On June 23, 1964, Byron De La Beckwith was arrested for Evers' murder. Twice that year, all-white juries deadlocked on De La Beckwith's guilt. The murder and the subsequent trials caused a public uproar. In 1994, thirty years after the two previous trials had failed to reach a verdict, De La Beckwith was again brought to trial, based on new evidence. He was convicted of murder on February 5, 1994, after having lived as a free man for the three decades following the killing. De La Beckwith appealed unsuccessfully, and died in prison in January 2001.

Assignments

1. Characterize "the white man" and his life, taking into consideration the aspects that the song depicts as well as the extra information at the end. (Orientation)
2. What stylistic devices are employed that underline the song's message and its specific character of being a political protest song? (Analysis)
3. You have a choice here. Choose **one** of the following tasks:
   - **3.1** Comment on the given song.
     Do you think that the reasons the song itself offers can be understood as a justification or an excuse? Which unspoken (political) demands are expressed in it? (Comment/Evaluation)
   - **3.2** As explained in the note attached to the poem, De La Beckwith appealed to the court.
     What arguments do you think he gave to the court/the jury to justify and explain his actions? Write his letter of appeal.
     ((Re-)creation of text)

Erwartungshorizont zu Klausur 1

zu 1: The "white man" committed a cowardly crime – shooting an innocent person from the back, while hiding behind a bush. Being underprivileged himself, he falls prey to the promises of the politicians who (ab-)use him for their own good. Right from the beginning of his life, he is instrumentalized: in order to make him an obedient tool that complies with the police's and politicians' wishes, he is told that the laws are with him, they protect him – he is taught that his hate is justified and right. Like the African-Americans, he is a victim himself: he is ordered to obey, to be subordinate, to hang and lynch, to be a merciless killer – in the name of the Ku Klux Klan. The "white man" is not treated like a human being – he is treated like a dog on a chain, obedient to and dependent on his master. Medgar Evers, as well as his white killer have something in common: both are only tools, pawns in a game that they cannot and do not control.

zu 2: The song describes the events in the style of a story or ballad and follows a clear chronological structure, told from a third person perspective. The language is colloquial with single elements of slang. When explaining the reason for the muddled situation, the speaker of the poem offers a very simple explanation that almost sounds like an excuse: "He (the white *and* the black man) is just a pawn in their game" – both are in a hopeless situation. The message of the song is that the ones who really are to blame are the Klan, the government, the politicians, the police – the "system" – but not the "killer". The song indirectly calls for actions against the government and for changing the system – it wants to make people aware of who is pulling the strings in the background. With its clear and critical political statement, its appeal to the people, its call for action – the song can be considered a protest song. However, the song is not aggressive nor does it call for people to be aggressive, but instead wants them to use their minds and not to believe everything they are told. The lyrics are easy to remember and to understand; there is a rather simply structured rhyme scheme (mostly pair rhymes) which also makes it a folk song that everybody can join in and sing along to.

zu 3.1: Most likely the students will argue that the reasons given cannot be considered an excuse but can be seen as an explanation – nevertheless, the killer was a grown man and therefore responsible for his actions. Unspoken political demands are that the system has to be changed in order to protect the people – the Whites and the Blacks – from dangerous demagogues who indoctrinate racist theories and hatred into poverty-stricken (white) Southerners who are an easy prey. Therefore, politics have to change and have to be changed by people who stand up to such ideologies.

zu 3.2:
- the students should use formal language and the style/design of a formal letter
- they should express that – as expressed in the song – De La Beckwith is sure of being protected by the law and certainly doesn't feel guilty about having committed a severe crime
- De La Beckwith could argue that he just did as he was told
- alternatively, De La Beckwith could resort to excuses, e.g. that Medgar Evers had provoked or threatened him and that his deed was merely an act of self-defense

Roger Cohen: Race and American memory

I was wandering through the King Center here when I stumbled on a movie clip of an indignant African-American woman saying: "If we can't live in our country and be accepted as free citizens and human beings, then something's the matter with something – and it isn't me."

That seemed a good, plain summation of the general conflict that has roiled American life since the nation's foundation, through slavery and segregation and their bitter legacies. When this anonymous woman spoke, less than a half-century ago, she was an unfree American. How she was schooled, where she could sit, and whom she could marry were matters determined by her race.

This "something's the matter with something – and it isn't me" is a big subject, the nation's "original sin", in Barack Obama's words. It's also a painful one that sees American ideals and practices at some remove from each other in ways of which Abu Ghraib was a reminder.

For nations to confront their failings is arduous. It involves what Germans, experts in this field, call *Geschichtspolitik*, or "the politics of history". It demands the passage from the personal to the universal, from individual memory to memorial. Yet there is as yet in the United States no adequate memorial for the ravages of race.

The King Center is a fine institution. But it's a modest museum, like others scattered through the country that deal with aspects of the nation's most divisive subject. Why, I wondered as I viewed the exhibit, does the Holocaust, a German crime, hold pride of place over U.S. lynchings in American memorialization?

Let's be clear: I am not comparing Jim Crow with industrialized mass murder, or suggesting an exact Klan-Nazi moral equivalency. But I do think some psychological displacement is at work when a magnificent Holocaust Memorial Museum, in which the criminals are not Americans, precedes a Washington institution of equivalent stature dedicated to the saga of national violence that is slavery and segregation.

I lived in Berlin for three years, a period spanning the Bundestag's decision in 1999 to build a Memorial to the Murdered Jews of Europe. The debate, 54 years after the collapse of Hitler's Reich, was fraught. It takes time to traverse the politics of history, confront guilt and arrive at an adequate memorialization of national crimes that also offers a possible path to reconciliation.

Germans have confronted the monstrous in them. In the end, they concluded the taint was so persuasive that Degussa, which was linked to the company that produced Zyklon-B gas, was permitted to provide the anti-graffiti coating for the memorial. The truth can be brutal, but flight from it even more devastating.

America's heroic narrative of itself is still in flight from race. The decision, approved by Congress in 2003, to build the Smithsonian's National Museum of African American History and Culture, to open in 2015, reflects a desire to plug this hole in the nation's memory. But what this $ 500 million institution will be remains to be invented. "The Holocaust is a horribly difficult subject, but the bad guys are not Americans," Lonnie Bunch, the museum's director, told me.

"Race, however, is the quintessential American story and one that calls into question how America defines itself and how we, as Americans, accept our own culpability."

He continued: "I am confident that the U.S. public can now do that. My challenge is to express not only the lynching, but also the resiliency and spirituality that are part of the core American identity." I also think America's ready, a half-century after the Civil Rights Movement, for this painful memorialization. But it won't be easy. The aborted International Freedom Center museum at ground zero, conceived to showcase liberty but dismissed by some as camouflage for a liberal agenda, shows how explosive the politics of history are.

"Memory", the French historian Pierre Nora noted, "is life." As such, it's subject to violent swings. [...]

indignant feeling and showing anger

to roil *ärgern, trüben*

Abu Ghraib US military prison, 20 miles west of Baghdad, where Iraqi detainees were abused and tortured by US military personnel

arduous involving a lot of effort and energy

the ravages of sth the destruction caused by sth

divisive causing people to split into groups that oppose each other

to precede to happen before sth

stature here: importance

fraught tense

to traverse to cross an area

reconciliation an end to disagreement and the start of a good relationship again

Degussa a global concern that operates in areas of speciality chemicals; founded in 1873 in Frankfurt/M., it is now based in Essen, Germany

to plug here: to provide sth missing

culpability the ability to feel responsible for or deserving of blame for having done sth wrong

resiliency here: the ability of people to feel better quickly after sth unpleasant

core most important, essential

camouflage here: behaviour that is deliberately meant to hide the truth

It's time for the country to ask itself some hard post-jingoistic questions and allow the memorialization of its darkest chapters. To demand truth commissions of other nations, while evading them at home, is unhelpful.

In committing to a major museum of African American History, and propelling the first serious African-American presidential candidate, the United States is recasting the psychology of its power. That's scary. It can also be salutary.

(719 words)

jingoistic believing strongly that your own country is best
to evade here: to avoid dealing with sth
to propel to move forward in a particular direction

International Herald Tribune, www.iht.com/articles/2008/04/16/opinion/edcohen.php [23.07.2008]

Assignments

1. Outline in which way the author of the given article, Roger Cohen, demonstrates the chances and risks for the Americans of accepting their own culpability by creating an "adequate memorial for the ravages of race" (l. 17). (Orientation)

2. Point out and explain the stylistic and rhetorical devices that create the argumentative character of this article. (Analysis)

3. Comment on and evaluate:
Viewing the text from a German perspective, do you share the author's opinion that
a) the Germans have been successful in transforming "individual memory to memorial" (l. 16)?
b) by building a major museum of African-American history, and propelling the first serious African-American presidential candidate, the United States is recasting the "psychology of its power" (ll. 57 f.)?
(Comment/Evaluation)

Erwartungshorizont zu Klausur 2

zu 1:

Chances	Risks
• slavery and segregation should have an institution of equivalent stature to the Holocaust • to tackle the nation's most divisive subject • an adequate memorialization of national crimes offers a path to reconciliation (→ Germany) • to fulfill the desire to plug the hole in the nation's memory • race is the quintessential American story • accepting culpability helps America to define itself • memory is life	• it is a painful subject that sees American ideals and practices at some remove from each other • being confronted with failings is arduous • truth can be brutal, but flight from it can be more devastating • politics of history are explosive • memory is subject to violent swings • demanding something from other nations but evading it at home is unhelpful

zu 2:

- referring to positive examples (→ German *Geschichtspolitik*)
- referring to one of the worst crimes ever committed, the Holocaust, indirectly recalls memories of how the Americans then confronted the German population with it
- explaining the chances that the confrontation with guilt offers
- alluding to the American hubris by demanding something from other nations that the Americans themselves avoid dealing with (→ weakness, lack of credibility)
- employing rhetorical questions to emphasize the inconsistency
- direct appeal to the readers
- a recapitulatory conclusion at the end

zu 3: Of course, different answers and views are possible here. However, the students should be able to explain their point of view and back it up with arguments and examples from German history and their personal experiences. They might refer to the aspect that, for the younger generation nowadays, it is much easier to deal with the German past than it used to be, for example, for their parents. It is simply a matter of fact that Germany and Germans committed horrible crimes in the past – it is part of German history that can be openly discussed. The Americans should consider the discussion about racism and segregation as a chance for reconciliation and as a long overdue occasion for talking with each other.

Konzeption des Unterrichtsmodells

Das vorliegende Unterrichtsmodell bietet einen Einblick in die amerikanische Bürgerrechtsbewegung, schwerpunktmäßig dargestellt am Beispiel von Liedern von afro-amerikanischen Interpreten wie Billie Holiday, Nina Simone oder Louis Armstrong wie auch klassischen Protestsongs von Bob Dylan oder Pete Seeger. Die einzelnen *Components* setzen jeweils unterschiedliche Akzente, die auch unabhängig voneinander oder einzeln – in Ergänzung zu dem zentralabiturrelevanten Thema *The American South* – betrachtet werden können. Die durch das Lied *Strange Fruit* bedingte Auseinandersetzung mit der Thematik *lynching* stellt neben dem Aspekt *slavery* eines der dunkelsten und grausamsten Kapitel der *history of African-Americans in the USA* dar und ist damit bis heute ein neuralgischer Punkt.

Component 1 stellt das Lied *Strange Fruit* in den Mittelpunkt sowie Reaktionen und Augenzeugenberichte aus dieser Zeit, den 1930er-Jahren. Dabei wird zunächst ein kreativer Ansatz gewählt, um sich dem schwierigen Thema zu nähern. Ergänzend können die Schülerinnen und Schüler Wortschatzarbeit zum Themenbereich *emotions* leisten und erhalten durch *Copy 3* (S. 24) und *Copy 17* (S. 52) methodisches Handwerkszeug, das ihnen hilft, sich mit Lyrik und Songtexten analytisch auseinanderzusetzen. Darüber hinaus bietet der Component verschiedene Textsorten und Medien an (YouTube Videoclip, Audio-CD, ein Munch-Gemälde), die unterschiedliche visuelle und auditive Zugänge zu der Thematik ermöglichen. Über eine Internetrecherche erarbeiten sich die Schüler historische und politische Hintergründe zur Entstehung des Liedes sowie des gesellschaftlichen Umfeldes der Sängerin Billie Holiday und des Komponisten und Texters Lewis Allan.

Neben Sängern und Songtextern haben sich auch andere Künstler mit dem Thema *lynching* auseinandergesetzt. ***Component 2*** bietet eine Auswahl von Gedichten aus der Phase der *Harlem renaissance* und den 1940er-Jahren, die in sehr unterschiedlicher Weise auf die Täter und die Opfer schauen. Auch die Short Story von Erskine Caldwell behandelt zwar dasselbe Thema, die Willkür der weißen Südstaatler, jedoch wird hier in fast selbstverständlicher Emotionslosigkeit der Mechanismus im Verhalten von weißem „Master" und schwarzem Plantagenbewohner beschrieben. Die Schüler erhalten über einen Sachtext erste Einblicke in historische und soziale Bedingungen und Zusammenhänge für Rassismus und Lynchmorde in den USA. Auch dies wird durch Internetrecherche vertieft und durch die Analyse von Statistiken faktisch untermauert. An authentischen Fällen, den Lynchmorden an Medgar Evers und Emmett Till sowie dem Bombenanschlag auf eine Kirche in Birmingham, wird untersucht, wie Liedermacher dies künstlerisch umgesetzt haben. Abschließend wird in einem Artikel des *Observers* der aktuelle Stand der Diskussion erörtert, die Forderung nach einer Entschuldigung und Wiedergutmachung wie auch die Wiederaufnahme von Gerichtsverfahren seit den 1990er-Jahren. Dieser *Component* kann auch zum Einstieg in das Thema genutzt werden, sodass die Schüler zunächst einen historisch-politischen Überblick erhalten und *dann* den Songtext *Strange Fruit* bearbeiten.

Copy 15 (S. 49) in ***Component 3*** bietet einen schlaglichtartigen Einstieg in die Ära der Bürgerrechtsbewegung, auch hier in Verbindung mit einem kreativen Ansatz und Internetrecherche. Der *Component* enthält weitere Songtexte, zum einen eine kleine Auswahl von „Klassikern" dieser Epoche, wie *We shall overcome,* zum anderen drei weitere Texte zur Thematik *racism* und *segregation.* Das *Analysis sheet* auf *Copy 17* (S. 52) bietet den Schülerinnen und Schülern Kriterien zur Bewertung und Analyse von Songtexten an und kann für alle im Unterrichtsmodell enthaltenen Songtexte genutzt werden.

Component 1

The song *Strange Fruit* and its background

Component 1 beschäftigt sich schwerpunktmäßig mit dem Song *Strange Fruit* und dem kulturellen und sozialgeschichtlichen Hintergrund seiner Entstehung. Über die ***Getting-started-Seite,*** auf OHP-Folie kopiert, können sich die Schülerinnen und Schüler dem Thema zunächst assoziativ nähern. Dabei sollte das *lynching*-Foto abgedeckt sein, sodass der Magnolienbaum/die Magnolienblüte im Mittelpunkt steht. Je nach Jahreszeit kann der Lehrer auch eine oder mehrere frische Magnolienblüten oder einen Zweig mit Blüten mitbringen und dem Kurs als (stillen) Impuls und Auftakt zu einem Brainstorming zeigen.

What do you associate with these flowers/trees?

spring, fragility, freshness, beauty, scent, innocence, new life, warmth, softness, etc.

Ergänzend kann nun der Song *Magnolia* von J. J. Cale vorgespielt werden (**CD, Track 6**). Man kann die Schüler bitten, beim Zuhören die Augen zu schließen und die Atmosphäre des Liedes auf sich wirken zu lassen. Die Eindrücke werden anschließend ergänzend zu den ersten Bemerkungen hinzugefügt.

Close your eyes and listen to the song *Magnolia* by J. J. Cale.
Which images and associations come to your mind?
What do you smell?

relaxation, summer, easygoing, chilling, holidays, New Orleans → "The Big Easy", jazz music, dancing, love, tenderness, the smell of blossoms, etc.

Als möglicher weiterer Gesprächsanlass kann auch diese „Definition" dienen.

> The majestic **magnolia tree** is indigenous to the South, having spread its deep roots in our rich soil for centuries. The magniola is a wide and solid tree, with large waxy leaves that provide so much shade that even the hardiest Southern grass has trouble thriving beneath its limbs. But despite its grand strength and powerful presence, the magnolia tree produces some of the most delicate, fragrant white flowers around. They provide shade, privacy, and an intoxicating scent. The Southern magnolia tree is the state tree of Mississippi and produces the state flower of both Mississippi and Louisiana. Magnolias stand as a symbol of all that is good about the South. They're found all over the country – wherever the conditions are right. They symbolize beauty, perseverance, strength, and patience.
>
> From: Deborah Ford, The Grits Guide to Life, Plume Publishing, New York 2003, pp. 5 ff.

Schließlich sollte auch das *lynching*-Foto auf der OHP-Folie aufgedeckt werden. Die Schüler werden in Gruppen mit zwei oder drei Schülern aufgeteilt; jede Gruppe erhält 4–5 Blätter Papier (evtl. auf die Form einer Sprechblase zugeschnitten).

Take a close look at the photo showing a lynching scene, and pay attention to details. Choose 2 – 3 of the by-standers, imagine their thoughts and write them down on the slips of paper. Then put the slips up on the board.

Die an der Tafel befestigten Sprechblasen werden dann im Plenum besprochen und bei Bedarf erklärt und ergänzt. Sollten die Schüler nicht von sich aus auf diesen Aspekt eingehen, kann auch vom Lehrer als Impuls die Frage gestellt werden:

Why do you think (some) people are having fun?

Als abschließende Hausaufgabe erhalten die Schüler eine Kopie der *Getting-started*-Seite und beantworten in schriftlicher Form die auf das *lynching*-Foto bezogenen Fragen.

1.1 A song about lynching

In der Folgestunde sollte im Anschluss an die Besprechung der Hausaufgaben nach Möglichkeit der Computerraum benutzt werden.
Auf der YouTube-Website www.youtube.com/watch?v=h4ZyuULy9zs können die Schüler einen Ausschnitt (2:33 Min.) des von Billie Holiday vorgetragenen Songs *Strange Fruit* anschauen bzw. anhören. Dabei sollten sie in Partnerarbeit Notizen zu ihren ersten Eindrücken von dem Lied selbst, aber auch von der Darstellung Holidays machen.

1. Watch the YouTube video and listen to the song *Strange Fruit.*
   What (in general) is the song about?
   What is your impression of the performance by Billie Holiday?
   What do you like/dislike about it?
2. Visit the website http://en.wikipedia.org/wiki/The_Scream and look at the famous picture *The Scream* painted by the Norwegian artist Edvard Munch, and find out about its message.
   What emotion does the painting aim to express?
3. Many critics have compared Billie Holiday's performances of *Strange Fruit* to the expressionist and nightmarish painting by Edvard Munch. Say why you (don't) share their opinion.

Billie Holiday performing *Strange Fruit*

Edvard Munch's painting *The Scream* (1893)

Strange Fruit

Southern trees bear a strange fruit,
Blood on the leaves and blood at the root,
Black body swinging in the Southern breeze,
Strange fruit hanging from the poplar trees.

Pastoral scene of the gallant South,
The bulging eyes and the twisted mouth,
Scent of magnolia sweet and fresh,
And the sudden smell of burning flesh!

Here is a fruit for the crows to pluck,
For the rain to gather, for the wind to suck,
For the sun to rot, for a tree to drop,
Here is a strange and bitter crop.

The lynching of Jim Redmond, Gus Roberson, and Bob Addison, May 17, 1892, Georgia

"There were stories about white people fighting among themselves for the dead man's fingers or toes, or pickling his penis and keeping it in a jar of the local barbershop. Or stories of white people putting on their Sunday best to attend lynchings, or even their uniforms from World War I or the Spanish-American War, as if racism was real patriotism: 'I am a real American. I lynch black folks. I keep them in their places'."

Vernon Jarrett, in: David Margolick, Strange Fruit, Philadelphia, Running Press, 2000, pp. 60f.

"An eye-witness to the lynching [...] said that [Claude] Neal had been forced to mutilate himself before he died. The eye-witness gave the following account of the event which took place in a swamp beside the Chattahoochee River:
[...] First they cut off his penis. He was made to eat it. Then they cut off his testicles and made him eat them and say he liked it. Then they sliced his sides and stomach with knives and every now and then somebody would cut off a finger or toe. Red hot irons were used on the nigger to burn him from top to bottom. From time to time during the torture a rope would be tied around Neal's neck and he was pulled over a limb and held there until he almost choked to death, when he would be let down and the torture begun all over again. After several hours of this punishment, they decided just to kill him. Neal's body was tied to a rope on the rear of an automobile and dragged over the highway to the Cannidy home. Here a mob estimated to number somewhere between 3,000 and 7,000 people from eleven southern states was excitedly waiting his arrival. [...] A woman came out of the Cannidy house and drove a butcher knife into his heart. Then the crowd came by and some kicked him and drove their cars over him. What remained of the body was brought by the mob to Marianna, where it is now hanging from a tree on the northeast corner of the courthouse square. Photographers say that they will soon have pictures of the body for sale at fifty cents each. Fingers and toes from Neal's body are freely exhibited on street-corners there."

A newspaper report about a lynching in Florida, 1934; quoted from: Ralph Ginzburg, One Hundred Years of Lynching, NY, Lancer, 1969, p. 222

Possible solutions for *The scream* by Edvard Munch:

- the painting shows an agonized person against a blood red sky; the person's eyes are wide open, he is screaming or crying and at the same time holding his hands against his ears as if to protect himself against something from the outside; the colours of the painting, red, orange and dark blue, black and brown are threatening and alarming;
- in his diary, Munch described his inspiration for the painting, *"I was walking along a path with two friends – the sun was setting – suddenly the sky turned blood red – I paused, feeling exhausted, and leaned on the fence – there was blood and tongues of fire above the blue-black fjord and the city – my friends walked on, and I stood there trembling with anxiety – and I sensed an infinite scream passing through nature."*
- the original title given to the painting by Munch was *"The Cry of Nature"*

Die Zitate auf ***Copy 1*, S. 18** sind aus den 1930er-Jahren, also der Zeit, in der das Lied *Strange Fruit* entstanden ist und von Billie Holiday erstmals vorgetragen und dann auch sehr schnell fester Bestandteil ihres Repertoires wurde. Dies ist deshalb von Bedeutung, da es zum einen die große gesellschaftliche Diskrepanz innerhalb der USA dieser Zeit verdeutlicht (vor allem im Süden wurden Lynchmorde an Schwarzen nicht als Verbrechen betrachtet, im Kontrast dazu entstanden Protestlieder gegen soziales Unrecht), zum anderen auch den großen Mut belegt, den eine (afro-amerikanische) Sängerin wie Billie Holiday haben musste, um einen solchen Song öffentlich vorzutragen. In Mobile, Alabama, wurde Billie Holiday aus der Stadt gejagt, als sie versuchte, das Lied vorzutragen. Auch der Süden selbst erscheint als äußerst widersprüchlich: Einerseits hängt man dem Ideal des *Old South* nach, in dem Kavaliere ihre Damen, *Southern Belles,* galant zu Bällen und anderen gesellschaftlichen Anlässen geleiteten und wo auf gesellschaftliche Etikette Wert gelegt wurde. Auf der anderen Seite aber gab es auch diese unvorstellbare Brutalität gegenüber den meist afro-amerikanischen Opfern, oft der verblendeten Idee folgend, eben diesen „Ehren- und Sittenkodex" zu verteidigen. Unter direkter oder indirekter Einflussnahme des Ku Klux Klans, der Mitglieder auch in den höchsten gesellschaftlichen Positionen hatte, konnten die Täter sicher sein, nicht (ernsthaft) gerichtlich belangt zu werden.
Nachdem die Schüler *Copy 1* bekommen und jeder für sich die Texte gelesen haben, ist es sinnvoll, zunächst kurz im Plenum erste Reaktionen und Eindrücke auszutauschen.
An dieser Stelle bietet sich an, die Schüler eine Art Kaleidoskop der Emotionen in Form von unterschiedlichen Wortfeldern zusammenstellen zu lassen. Dazu sollten Wörterbücher bereitgestellt werden (der Kurs kann auch in kleine Gruppen zu je 3–4 Schülern aufgeteilt werden). Die Ergebnisse können von den Schülern entweder an der Tafel oder aber auch auf OHP-Folie festgehalten werden (oder verschiedenen Folien). Diese Übung ist zum einen eine gute Wortschatzübung, zum anderen bereitet sie die anschließende Hausaufgabe vor.

What do you consider (the different) people's emotions to be while/after lynching somebody?
Use your dictionary to find as many adjectives as possible in order to reflect the variety of emotions (based on the variety of people) that people have concerning lynching.
Then write these adjectives on the board in different categories, e.g.:
positive ... indifferent ... negative attitude ...
enthusiastic ... neutral ... disgusted ...
frightened ... confused ... aggressive ...

Mögliches Tafelbild/Wortfelder zu *describing emotions:*

positive	**indifferent**	**negative**	**enthusiastic**	**neutral**
glad content cheerful amused lively excited carefree interested curious …	shy timid hesitant uncertain uneasy uncomfortable indecisive …	miserable depressed agitated nervous anxious sad worried concerned …	boisterous exuberant eager keen in high spirits …	unconcerned without worrying bored uninvolved …
disgusted	**frightened**	**confused**	**aggressive**	**…**
annoyed unhappy …	desperate horrified agonized …	dismayed restless insecure obsequious tense rapt …	furious irritable touchy incited …	…

Eine die Thematik abschließende Hausaufgabe könnte sein:

Imagine you were one of the people watching the lynching scene described in the newspaper. Choose one perspective and write a diary entry about what you witnessed. Describe the situation, your thoughts and emotions. You are:

a) a member of the Klan,
b) an Afro-American,
c) a "lynching tourist" from the South where lynching is rather common,
d) a "lynching tourist" from the North where lynching is rather uncommon.

Hier sind unterschiedliche Lösungen denkbar; wichtig ist, dass die Schülerinnen und Schüler wirklich versuchen, sich in die jeweilige Rolle hineinzuversetzen.
In dieser Unterrichtsstunde (am besten eine Doppelstunde) soll nun der Song selbst im Mittelpunkt stehen. Die **CD** hält neben der Originalversion von Billie Holiday noch weitere Interpretationen von *Strange Fruit* bereit. Die Schüler sollten die Kopien des Songtextes sowie je vier Kopien von ***Copy** 17,* **S. 52** erhalten, auf denen sie die Höreindrücke festhalten.

Listen to the various different interpretations of *Strange Fruit* and take notes while listening.

1. Billie Holiday (1939)
2. Cassandra Wilson (1995)
3. Sting (1997)
4. UB40 (1980)

Im Anschluss daran werden die Ergebnisse im Plenum besprochen und stichwortartig an der Tafel festgehalten. Mögliches Tafelbild:

Billie Holiday	**Cassandra Wilson**	**Sting**	**UB40**
• introduction only instrumental (1:10) • trumpet, piano • melodious • like (soft) background music in a bar • sung ballad-like • soft gentle voice, like velvet	• dramatic instrumental introduction (bass, trumpet, guitar) • dramatic, very dark voice • music sometimes is tuneless • instrumental intersections after each stanza • ghostly • very jazzy	• trumpet, percussion • almost big band sound, orchestral • voice sounds doleful and sorrowful • emphasis on last word of each verse • saxophone • song gets more jazz-like • repetition of the terms "Strange Fruit" and "Southern Trees" • sound gets more and more dramatic and haunting	• instrumental introduction: the leitmotif played by a trumpet • percussion, keyboards • reggae-like sound and rhythm • melodious voice • instruments dominate; voice is rather quiet • rhythmical, swinging music • saxophone • break after: "fruit" • abrupt ending
→ strong contrast to the threatening lyrics	→ instrumentation and voice match the lyrics	→ dramatically rising to a kind of climax	→ strong contrast to the lyrics

Die auf ***Copy 2, S. 22*** gesammelten Reaktionen auf die Billie-Holiday-Interpretation des Liedes kann an dieser Stelle für weitere Diskussions-*incentives* dienen.
Für das Gespräch ließen sich auch folgende weitere Fragen denken:

- In what way do the lyrics of *Strange Fruit* reflect and incorporate the multi-layered and complex situation of the American South?
- How have the versions changed?
- How do these changes influence the atmosphere and message of the song?
- What version do you consider the most/least appropriate one?
- How would you yourself interpret the song?
  Could you imagine a RAP version?

In einem musikalisch sehr interessierten Kurs kann man die Schüler auch eine neue, noch zeitgemäßere Version selbst erstellen und vorführen lassen. Alternativ kann man in technisch versierten Kursen auch einen oder mehrere (für jede der Versionen) Video-Clips herstellen lassen, indem z. B. Bilder aus den Südstaaten, aus *Gone with the wind, Mississippi burning, lynching*-Fotos etc. eingearbeitet werden. Auch hier ist der Fantasie der Schülerinnen und Schüler keine Grenze gesetzt.

Make a video clip in which you employ one (or more) version(s) of the soundtrack of *Strange Fruit* in the background.
You can also employ scenes from famous movies like *Gone with the wind* or *Mississippi burning* for your video clip.

Reactions to *Strange Fruit*

"Why don't you sing that sexy song you're so famous for? ... You know, the one about the naked bodies swinging in the trees?"

a female fan in a night club, from: Billie Holiday, Lady Sings the Blues, London, Penguin, 2005, p. 84

"A prime piece of musical propaganda for the NAACP."

TIME, May 1939

"Witnessing *Strange Fruit* at Café Society was a visual, as well as an auditory, experience. [...]
Before she began, all service was stopped. Waiters, cashiers, busboys were all immobilized. The room went completely dark, save for a pin spot on Holiday's face. When she was finished and the lights went out, she was to walk off the stage, and no matter how thunderous the ovation, she was never to return for a bow. ... the waiters made a habit of going up to the noisiest characters and saying: 'Miss Holiday is afraid you aren't enjoying yourself. Pay up and go.'"

David Margolick

"When I heard her sing I heard other kinds of lynchings, not just hanging from trees. I saw my own mother and father, two college-educated people, and all the crap they had to go through. Only three white men ever called my father 'Mister', and one of them later acted as though it was a mistake. To me, that was part of the whole lynch syndrome, the lynching of the body and the spirit put together."

Vernon Jarrett

"They'd never heard anything remotely like this ... never even heard anyone speaking about lynching. I remember one girl just broke down and started sobbing. It was propagandizing, spreading the word. It made an impact on people. For the first time in their lives it made them think about the lynching victims as humans, as people."

Warren Morse

"I played it over and over to get a better perspective on what type of world I was living in. I play it a lot now. It helps me understand that there are ignorant people in the world, and it allows me to have pity for their ignorance."

Morgan Monceaux

"If the anger of the exploited ever mounts high enough in the South, it now has its Marseillaise."

Samuel Grafton, *New York Post*

"Anti-Lynch Propaganda in Swingtime on a disc."

Variety, May 1939

"Sometimes perfection happens, and this was one of those times ... the perfect horror described in a voice which could encompass horror without apparent effort or strain, making it far more indelible than the dramatic emphasis of opera ...
Still, I have to wonder if she truly understood the power of "Strange Fruit". To bring into the world of swinging, light-hearted or blues-like jazz a song about the deepest shame of the racist America was like inviting your neighborhood murderer to your Fourth of July barbecue and expecting your friends to accept him as just another guest, and the occasion as just another day in their lives."

Frances Rowe, jazz aficionado, in the late 1950s

Im Anschluss an den Vergleich der verschiedenen *Strange-Fruit*-Versionen ergibt sich die folgende Hausaufgabe, bei der die Schüler ihre Notizen von *Copy 17* nutzen sollten. Sollen die Schüler stärker interpretierend arbeiten, kann man ihnen auch ***Copy 3,* S. 24** als Hilfestellung an die Hand geben.

Write your personal statement on the song *Strange Fruit.*
In writing a review, pay attention to the different interpretations performed at different times as well as to stylistic aspects concerning the instrumentation and the vocals.

1.2 The songwriter and the original performer

***Copy 4,* S. 25** bietet kurze Hintergrundinformationen zu Lewis Allan, dem Texter und Komponisten von *Strange Fruit,* sowie zu Billie Holiday, die das Lied als Erste gesungen hat. Beide eignen sich thematisch sehr gut für weitere Recherchearbeit oder aber als Themen für Projekte oder Facharbeiten. Sehr gute Informationen hierzu bietet der Film *Strange Fruit* von Joel Katz aus dem Jahr 2002 (siehe Anhang). Die folgenden Websites bieten vielseitige weitere Informationen:

- www.metascholar.org/MOSC/essays/meeropol.htm (u.a. auch die Noten zum Lied)
- www.cpa.org.au/garchve03/1136cult.html (ein Artikel aus dem *Guardian,* May 7, 2003)
- www.guardian.co.uk/books/2007/aug/18/jazz.urban/print (ein weiterer Artikel aus dem *Guardian* aus 2007)

1. Do research on Lewis Allan and Billie Holiday, and find out more about the origin of the song and the courage of the people who spoke out against the injustice and crime and of lynching.
2. Prepare a presentation and a wall poster to inform your class about
   a) Billie Holiday,
   b) Lewis Allan.

1.3 Political cabaret and jazz clubs in Harlem and Greenwich Village

Das *Café Society* in Greenwich Village, New York, wurde 1938 eröffnet und war eine Mischung aus Nightclub und Kabarett, allerdings mit stark politischer Ausrichtung. Es sollte ein Lokal für die „normalen" Leute sein und kein *Upper Class Club,* worin sich auch die politisch linke Ausrichtung des Inhabers Barney Josephson widerspiegelt. Im Gegensatz zu vielen Jazz Clubs in Harlem, in denen Rassentrennung praktiziert wurde (zwar waren die Künstler Afro-Amerikaner, die Besucher waren jedoch ausschließlich meist gut betuchte Weiße), wurden im *Café Society* keine Rasseschranken gemacht. Hier spielte natürlich auch der politisch-kulturelle Geist von Greenwich Village eine entscheidende Rolle, das berühmt war für seine Künstler und seine politisch kritische und kulturell avantgardistische Haltung. Dort war gewissermaßen eine der „Brutstätten" der späteren Bürgerrechtsbewegung. ***Copy 5,* S. 26** bietet hierzu einige Einstiegsinformationen, die als Ausgangspunkt für eine weitere Recherche dienen können. In diesem Zusammenhang bietet sich als Projekt auch der Roman sowie der gleichnamige Film *Ragtime* von E. L. Doctorow an, der vor der Kulisse der Clubs im New York der 1920er-Jahre das Schicksal des afro-amerikanischen Musikers Coalhouse Walker in seinem Streben nach sozialer Gerechtigkeit darstellt.

Analysis of lyrics and poetry

Poetry (from the Greek "poiesis" = making, creating) is a type of literature in which ideas, experiences and feelings are expressed in compact, imaginative, often musical language. Poets arrange words in ways designed to touch readers' senses, emotions and minds. Lyrics are a set of words that accompany music, either by speaking or singing. The word *lyric* derives from the Greek word "lyrikos" (= a song sung by the lyre). Most poems and lyrics are written in lines that may contain patterns of rhyme and rhythm to help convey their meaning. They often use figures of speech and imagery to appeal to the readers' and listeners' emotions and imagination. The poet or songwriter usually invents a speaker from whose point of view s/he expresses feelings, ideas, experiences, etc. Poems and songs may be divided into stanzas (groups of lines) or sections and can greatly vary in structure, theme and atmosphere.

General meaning/ content:	• What situation/topic is presented? • What is the theme; are there any (striking) leitmotifs? • What is the author's/singer's intention; what is the message of the poem/song? • What kind of register of English has been chosen (poetic, colloquial, archaic, slang, etc.)? • What is the melody like (melodious, rhythmical, tuneful, staccato, etc.)?
Formal analysis: a) structural devices:	• How is the poem/song structured (stanzas, lines, (lack of) punctuation, refrain(s), break(s), enjambments, chorus, etc.)? • use of repetitions and/or enumerations/parallelisms • use of contrast(s)/antithesis • use of an illustration (= an example to make an idea clear) • rhyme scheme (e.g. pair rhyme aa bb cc …; cross rhyme abab; enclosed rhyme abba) • free verse
b) sense devices:	• How are objects and ideas/thoughts brought together? • What type(s) of sentence(s) is/are used (hypotactical/paratactical sentences, questions, commands, etc.)? • allusions/references to a certain topic (e.g. nature, city, love, etc.) • use of simile (a direct comparison, "like, as"); metaphor (an implied comparison without a connective word: "an ocean of tears); a personification (something non-human is given human characteristics: "the frosty cliffs looked cold"); symbol (an object that also stands for some abstract idea: a red rose → symbol of love, beauty) • use of grammatical tenses • point of view • hyperbole/exaggeration
c) sound devices:	• use of alliteration/anaphora • use of rhymes and/or assonances (= imperfect rhymes) • use of a particular rhythm, beat • onomatopeia (= words that imitate a sound: buzz, cuckoo, etc.) • instrumentation, beat, vocal/instrumental type of music, vocals, etc. → **Show how these devices support, stress/emphasize the meaning/content of the poem/song (→ function/effect).** → **Show how style and content are connected.** → **Show how sound and lyrics match and support each other.**
d) comment/ evaluation:	• Try to classify the given poem/song (refer to other poems/songs by the same author or authors of the same background). • Evaluate the poem/song (is the poem/song convincing?; has the author/singer succeeded in conveying his message?, etc.). • What do you consider to be the final message of the poem/song? • What do you consider to be the effect on the reader/listener?

Lewis Allan and Billie Holiday: the writer and the performer

Lewis Allan (alias Abel Meeropol)

Billie Holiday and her band

Holiday was born in Philadelphia on April 7, 1915. That made her only twenty-four years old in 1939, but she had already experienced enough prejudice and despair then – including time in a home for wayward back children, then in a whorehouse, where she first heard the recordings of Bessie Smith and Louis Armstrong – to call herself a "race woman". She began performing in Harlem in the late 1920s; by 1933, she had been discovered by the great record producer John Hammond, who quickly teamed her up with Benny Goodman, Teddy Wilson, and other legendary musicians of the day. [...] Though all of the hard knocks helped Holiday infuse a unique mixture of resilience, defiance, exuberance, and shrewdness into everything she sang, her songs, at least on paper, were invariably what her first biographer, Linda Kuehl, called "second cousins to her favorite reading: love comics and true romance magazines" – that is, bland, banal ballads. Politics, and particularly racial politics, had never influenced her choice of material until "Strange Fruit" came along. [...]
[Abel Meeropol] An English teacher at De Witt Clinton High School in the Bronx for twenty-seven years, he had led two other, parallel lives. One was a political activist: he and his wife were closet Communists, donating a percentage of their earnings to the Party ... [...] The other was as a writer, poet, and composer. [...] He wrote incessantly – poems, ballads, musicals, plays – all using the nom de plume "Lewis Allan", the names of his two natural-born children, neither of whom survived infancy. Many of his creations were political, albeit with a light touch ... [...]
... it is possible that what inspired him to write "Strange Fruit" was a double lynching that took place north of the Mason Dixon line – in Marion, Indiana, in 1930 – immortalized in a shocking and widely publicized photograph. In any case, it was around that time that Meeropol, then in his early thirties, came across in a civil rights magazine a photograph of a particularly ghastly lynching, and he said it had haunted him for days. So he wrote a poem about it, one that the Communist journal *The New Masses* agreed in early 1936 to publish but that saw first print – as "Bitter Fruit" – in the January 1937 issue of *The New York Teacher,* a union publication.
Meeropol often asked others, most notably Earl Robinson, to set his poems to music. But with "Strange Fruit", he insisted on doing the task himself.

The Café Society

HAVE YOU HEARD?

"Strange fruit growing on Southern trees"

sung by

BILLIE HOLIDAY

at **CAFE SOCIETY**

2 Sheridan Square • CHelsea 2-2737

"The wrong place for the Right people"

Ad in *The New Yorker*, 1939

Café Society, "a night club to take the stuffing out of stuffed shirts," where the left wing WPA [= Works Progress Administration] types [...] did the murals and a simian-looking Hitler hung from the ceiling by the coat check – was unusual for New York City. Dubbing itself "the wrong place for the Right people", it mocked the empty celebrity worship, right-wing politics, snootiness, and racial discrimination of popular New York hangouts like the Stork Club.
At Café Society the doormen wore rags and ragged white gloves and stood by as the customers opened the doors themselves; the bartenders were all veterans of the Abraham Lincoln Brigade; blacks and whites fraternized on stage and off. As one press account described it, the club had "no girlie line, no smutty gags, no Uncle Tom comedy." George Avakian, the famed record producer, wrote that "the café was one of the 'good' places in which Negroes were permitted, and, if possible, given the best tables, while anyone in evening clothes would be placed behind a pillar or almost in the kitchen." Its politics were somewhere left of the New Deal; when Eleanor Roosevelt made what might have been her only foray into a New York nightclub, it was to Café Society that she went. [...]
Café Society was the brainchild of Barney Josephson, a shoe salesman from Trenton, New Jersey, with progressive sympathies. Its patrons, the historian David Stowe has written, consisted of "labor leaders, intellectuals, writers, jazz lovers, celebrities, students and assorted leftists." As Michael Denning, an American Studies professor at Yale put it, Café Society represented a unique synthesis of cultures, blending the politically radical cabarets of Weimar, Berlin and Paris with the jazz clubs and revues of Harlem. In both its Village incarnation and at a second location in Midtown Manhattan, Café Society attracted people like Nelson Rockefeller, Charlie Chaplin, Errol Flynn, Lauren Bacall, Lillian Hellman, Langston Hughes ... [...] It was probably the only place in America where "Strange Fruit" could have been sung and performed.

Component 2

Lynching – historical and literary approaches

Lynching: Form of mob violence in which a mob executes a presumed offender, often also torturing him and mutilating his body, without trial, under the pretense of administering justice. The term "lynch law" refers to a self-constituted court that imposes sentence on a person without due process of law. Both terms are derived from the name of Charles Lynch, a Virginia planter and patriot who, during the American Revolution, headed an irregular court formed to punish Loyalists.

From: Encyclopaedia Britannica, Vol. 7, p. 589

Component 2 bietet verschiedene Textsorten sowie Statistiken zum Themenbereich *lynching.* Methodisch ist auch denkbar, mit diesem *Component* in die Reihe einzusteigen, um den Schülerinnen und Schülern zunächst ein gewisses Faktenwissen zu vermitteln, bevor sie sich mit dem Songtext selbst beschäftigen. Hierzu erhalten die Schüler zunächst Sachinformationen in Form eines Textes der Yale University sowie mehrere Statistiken, die das Ausmaß der Lynchmorde belegen. In Ergänzung dazu finden sich auf der Website www.spartacus.schoolnet.co.uk/USAlynching.htm eine Vielzahl weiterer Informationen und Links zum Thema, die sich hervorragend zur weiteren Recherche für Projekte oder Facharbeiten eignen.
In (den Auszügen) der *Short Story* „The end of Christy Tucker" von Erskine Caldwell wird die Brutalität eines (weißen) Plantagenbesitzers dargestellt, der seinen (schwarzen) *Sharecropper* erschießt, weil er sich von ihm provoziert fühlt.
Schließlich soll an einem authentischen Fall, der Ermordung von Emmett Till im Jahre 1955, gezeigt werden, in welcher Weise weiße wie afro-amerikanische Künstler dieses *lynching* in ihren Liedern verarbeitet haben. Der Artikel aus dem *Observer* vom Juni 2005 schließlich zeigt, dass dieses Kapitel amerikanischer Geschichte keineswegs abgeschlossen ist und seine Schatten bis in die Gegenwart wirft.

2.1 The historical background of lynching

Als Einstieg in diesen Themenschwerpunkt sollten die Schülerinnen und Schüler zunächst über mögliche Ursachen für Lynchmorde nachdenken und spekulieren:

> Between 1882 and 1968 almost five thousand people were lynched in the USA, most of them in the South.
> Speculate on possible reasons that may have caused all these murders that were mostly committed against Afro-Americans.

Mögliches Tafelbild:

Possible reasons for lynching

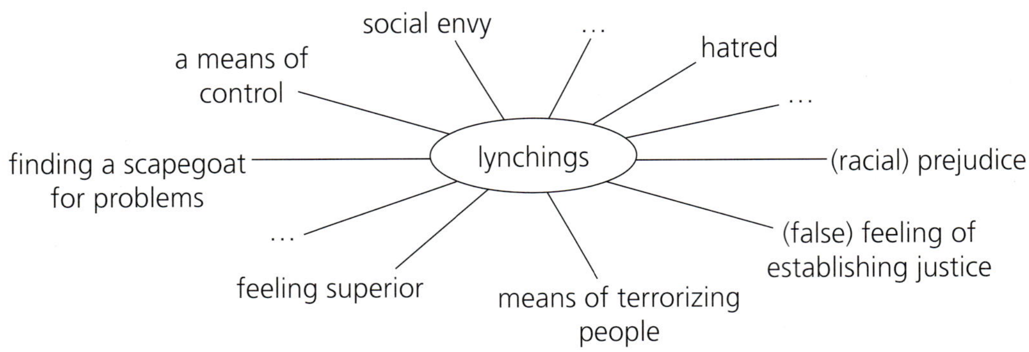

Durch die Bearbeitung von ***Copy 6*, S. 29** und ***Copy 7*, S. 30** erlangen die Schüler weitere Einsicht in die Hintergründe von Lynchmorden. Die Schüler sollten zunächst *Copy 6* bearbeiten und dann in Ergänzung dazu die Statistiken auf *Copy 7*. Für die Bearbeitung der Statistik „Lynchings by year and race" ist es sinnvoll, als weiterführende Hausaufgabe die Hintergründe der Zeitangaben recherchieren zu lassen. Je nach zeitlicher Planung können diese Statistiken in Verbindung mit weiteren Rechercheaufgaben zur Historie sowie zu den aufgelisteten Staaten ein lohnendes Kursprojekt ergeben, das in einer gemeinsam erstellten Wandzeitung dokumentiert wird.

1. Read the information given on *Copy 6* and find out about the reasons for lynchings in the 19th and 20th century.
2. Be prepared to give a short speech on the basic reasons for the lynching of black people.
3. Comment on and explain W. E. DuBois' assumption that "… the white South feared more than Negro dishonesty, ignorance and incompetency, Negro honesty, knowledge and efficiency."
4. Analys… ven related t… as the causes…
5. Do res…
   a) the … py 7,
   b) the … isted in the …
   Togeth… display your fi…

(to) maim – jmd. verstümmeln
(to) indict sb. – jmd. anklagen
(to) sentence sb. – verurteilen
prosecutor – Staatsanwalt
uppity – dreist / hochnäsig

Zu erwar…

1. • lync… engenderi…
   • as a means of social control to sustain the caste system of the South
   • a combination of sadism and racism
   • most effective means of control: fear

Lynching in the 19th and 20th century

In the last decades of the nineteenth century, the lynching of Black people in the Southern and border states became an institutionalized method used by whites to terrorize Blacks and maintain white supremacy. In the South, during the period 1880 to 1940, there was a deep-seated and all-pervading hatred and fear of the Negro which led white mobs to turn to "lynch law" as a means of social control. Lynchings – open public murders of individuals suspected of crime conceived and carried out more or less spontaneously by a mob – seem to have been an American invention. [...]
Most of the lynchings were by hanging or shooting, or both. However, many were of a more hideous nature – burning at the stake, maiming, dismemberment, castration, and other brutal methods of physical torture. Lynching therefore was a cruel combination of racism and sadism, which was utilized primarily to sustain the caste system in the South. Many white people believed that Negroes could only be controlled by fear. To them, lynching was seen as the most effective means of control. [...]
Contrary to present-day popular conception, lynching was not a crime committed exclusively against Black people. During the nineteenth century a significant minority of the lynching victims were white. Between the 1830s and the 1850s the majority of those lynched in the United States were whites. Although a substantial number of white people were victims of this crime, the vast majority of those lynched, by the 1890s and after the turn of the century, were Black people. Actually, the pattern of almost exclusive lynching of Negroes was set during the Reconstruction period. [...]
Lynchings occurred most commonly in the smaller towns and isolated rural communities of the South where people were poor, mostly illiterate, and where there was a noticeable lack of wholesome community recreation. The people who composed mobs in such neighborhoods were usually small landholders, tenant farmers and common laborers, whose economic status was very similar to that of the Negro. They frequently found Black men economic competitors and bitterly resented any Negro progress. Their starved emotions made the raising of a mob a quick and simple process, and racial antagonism made the killing of Negroes a type of local amusement which broke the monotony of rural life. [...]
Lynching was a local community affair. When the sentiment of the community favored lynching, the laws were difficult or impossible to enforce. State authorities often attempted to prevent lynchings, but seldom punished the mob participants. Because of the tight hold on the courts by local public opinion, lynchers were rarely ever indicted by a grand jury or sentenced. The judge, prosecutor, jurors and witnesses – all white – were usually in sympathy with the lynchers. If sentenced, the participants in the lynch mobs were usually pardoned. [...] Myrdal suggests several background factors and underlying causes for the prevalence of lynching in rural areas by lower class whites: poverty, economic and social fear of the Negro, low level of education, and the "isolation, the dullness of every day life and the general boredom of rural and small town life." However, the fundamental cause of lynching was the fear of the Negro – the basis of racism and discrimination. Many Whites, after Reconstruction and during the first four decades of the twentieth century, feared that the Negro was "getting out of his place" and that the white man's social status was threatened and was in need of protection. Lynching was seen as the method to defend white domination and keep the Negroes from becoming "uppity". Therefore, lynching was more the expression of white American fear of Black social and economic advancement than of Negro crime. W.E.B. DuBois was correct when he stated: "... the white South feared more than Negro dishonesty, ignorance and incompetency, Negro honesty, knowledge, and efficiency."

http://www.yale.edu/ynhti/curriculum/units/1979/2/79.02.04.x.html [25.03.2008]

Lynching statistics

Lynchings by year and race

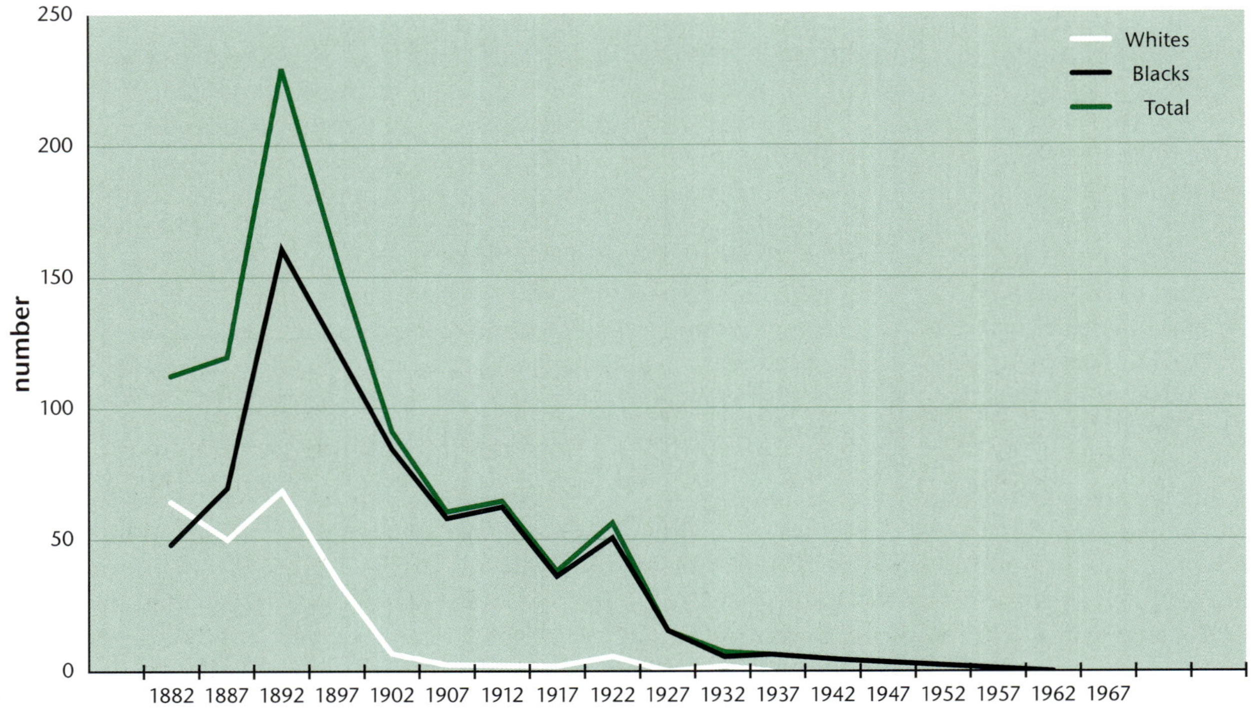

Total numbers: Whites 1,297 Blacks 3,446 Total 4,743

Lynchings by state and race (1882–1968)

State	Whites	Blacks	Total
Alabama	48	299	347
Arkansas	58	226	284
Florida	25	257	282
Georgia	39	492	531
Louisiana	56	335	391
Mississippi	42	539	581
North Carolina	15	86	101
South Carolina	4	156	160
Tennessee	47	204	251
Texas	141	352	493
Virginia	17	83	100
South Total	**492**	**3,029**	**3,521**
US Total	**1,297**	**3,446**	**4,743**

Causes of lynchings (1882–1968)

Causes	Number	%
Homicides	1,937	40.84
Felonious assault	205	4.32
Rape	912	19.22
Attempted rape	288	6.07
Robbery and theft	232	4.89
Insult to white person	85	1.79
All other reasons	1,084	22.85
Total	**4,743**	**100**

Data: Archives at the Tuskegee Institute; www.law.umkc.edu/faculty/projects/ftrials/shipp/lynchstats.html [25.03.2008]

- poverty and illiteracy of the white lynch mob
- social envy of small white landholders → competition to Blacks
- local amusement to break up the monotony of rural life → boredom
- laws against lynching were difficult or impossible to enforce
- lynchers were hardly ever sentenced
- the fear of the "Negro" getting out of control
- white fear of Black social and economic advancement

3.
   - as the white people from the countryside often felt disadvantaged themselves because of their lack of education and social status, they feared the advancement of the African-Americans who might become more successful, more educated, etc.
   - a "Negro" being dishonest and uneducated, or even criminal justified their cruel and brutal behaviour towards the Black population

4.
   - peak lynching numbers: 1882 until the 1900s (→ era of Reconstruction and its failure led to enormous social tensions, the introduction of segregation and an increase of racism)
   - only after 1905 and 1930 did the number of lynchings sink significantly (→ 1909 the NAACP was founded; → 1933–38 New Deal/ economic recovery; 1910–1940 The Great Migration: about 1.6 Million African-American migrants left the South to the North, Midwest and West to escape racism and find better opportunities; 1946 President Harry S. Truman established committee on Civil Rights)
   - not surprisingly, the most Blacks were lynched in the Southern states (3,029 out of 3,446 total); most of the "official" causes for lynchings were murder, rape and "all other reasons" – which is a significantly high number of obviously dubious reasons for lynching someone.

2.2 A short story about lynching

Die 1940 erschienene Short Story *The end of Christy Tucker* von Erskine Caldwell *(**Copy 8, S. 32f.**)* verdeutlicht die vollkommene Willkür und den absoluten Machtanspruch der Weißen in den Südstaaten, hier verkörpert durch den Plantagenbesitzer Lee Crossman und sein Opfer, den schwarzen Baumwoll-Pächter Christy. Christys Verhängnis ist seine offensichtliche Intelligenz und Geschäftstüchtigkeit – und sein Widerspruchsgeist. Er realisiert nicht, dass genau diese Eigenschaften ihn zum Objekt des Hasses und zum möglichen Konkurrenten werden lassen. In der Diskussion, die sich zwischen den beiden entspinnt, kann Crossman der Logik Christys schließlich nur seine gnadenlose und eiskalte Brutalität entgegensetzen: Er will ihn auspeitschen und als dieser sich auch diesmal zur Wehr setzt, erschießt er ihn „in Notwehr". Die zentrale Aussage dieser Geschichte entspricht genau dem, was W. E. B. DuBois äußerte: „... the white South feared ... Negro honesty, knowledge, and efficiency." (S. 29)

Die Schülerinnen und Schüler erhalten zunächst nur den ersten Teil der Geschichte (bis Zeile 74) ohne Angabe des Titels.

Erskine Caldwell: The end of Christy Tucker (part one)

Christy had moved to the Crossman plantation the first of the year. About three months before. It was the first time he had ever been in Georgia, and he had grown to like it better than Alabama, where he had always lived. He and his wife had decided to come to Georgia because they had heard that the land there was better for sharecropping cotton. Christy said that he could not be satisfied merely making a living; he wanted to get ahead in life.

Lee Crossman still had not come, and Christy sat down in one of the chairs. He had no more than seated himself when the door opened. He jumped to his feet.

"Howdy, Mr. Lee," he said, smiling.

"I've had a good chance to look at the land, and I'd like to be furnished with another mule and a gang plow. I figure a can raise twice as much cotton on that kind of land with a gang plow, because it's about the best I ever saw. There's not a rock or stump on it, and it's as clear of bushes as the palm of my hand. I haven't even found a gully anywhere on it. If you'll furnish me with another mule and a gang plow, I'll raise more cotton for you than any two sharecroppers on your plantation."

Lee Crossman listened until he had finished, and then he slammed the door shut and strode across in the room.

"I sent for you, nigger," he said. "You didn't send for me, did you?"

"That's right, Mr. Lee," he said. "You sent for me."

"Then keep your black face shut until I tell you to open it."

"Yes, sir, Mr. Lee," Christy said, backing across the room until he found himself against the wall. Lee Crossman sat down in a chair and glared at him.

"Yes, sir, Mr. Lee," Christy said again.

"You're one of these biggity niggers, ain't you?" Lee said. "Where'd you come from, anyway? You ain't a Georgia nigger, are you?"

"No, sir, Mr. Lee," Christy said, shaking his head. "I was born and raised in Alabama."

"Didn't they teach you any better than this in Alabama?"

"Yes, sir, Mr. Lee."

Christy wiped his face with the palm of his hand and wondered what Lee Crossman was angry with him about. He began to understand why the other Negroes had gone out of their way to keep from talking to him. They knew he had been sent for, and that meant he had done something to displease Lee Crossman. They did not wish to be seen talking to anyone who was in disfavor with the plantation owner and boss.

"Have you got a radio?" Lee asked.

"Yes, sir."

"Where'd you get it?"

"I bought it on time."

"Where'd you get the money to pay on it?"

"I had a little, and my wife raises a few chickens."

"Why didn't you buy it at the plantation store?"

"I made a better bargain at the other place. I got it a little cheaper."

"Niggers who live on my plantation buy what they need at my plantation store," Lee said.

"I didn't want to go into debt to you, Mr. Lee," Christy said. "I wanted to come out ahead when the accounts are settled at the end of the year."

Lee Crossman leaned back in the chair, crossed his legs, and took out his pocketknife. He began cleaning his fingernails. [...]

"Do you know what we do with biggity niggers like you in Georgia?"

"No, sir."

"We teach them to mind their own business and stay in their place."

Erskine Caldwell: The end of Christy Tucker (part two)

Lee Crossman got up and crossed the room to the closet. He jerked the door open and reached inside. When he turned around, he was holding a long leather strap studded with heavy brass brads. He came back across the room, slapping the strap around his boot tops.

"Who told your wife she could raise chickens on my plantation?" he said to Christy.

"Nobody told her, Mr. Lee," Christy said. "We didn't think you'd mind. There's plenty of yard around the house for them, and I built a little hen house."

"Stop arguing with me, nigger!"

"Yes, sir."

"I don't want chickens scratching up crops on this plantation."

"Yes, sir," Christy said.

"Where did you get money to pay on a radio?"

"I snared a few rabbits and skinned them, and then I sold their hides for a little money."

"I don't want no rabbits touched on my plantation," Lee said.

He shook out the heavy strap and cracked it against his boots.

"Why haven't you got anything down on the books in the plantation store?" Lee asked.

"I just don't like to go into debt," Christy said. "I want to come out ahead when the accounts are settled at the end of the year."

"That's my business whether you come out owing or owed at the end of the year," Lee said.

He pointed to a crack in the floor.

"Take off that shirt and drop your pants and get down on your knees astraddle that crack," the white man said.

"What are you going to do to me, Mr. Lee?"

"I'll show you what I'm going to do," he replied. "Take off that shirt and pants and get down there like I told you."

"Mr. Lee I can't let you beat me like that. No, sir, Mr. Lee. I can't let you do that to me. I just can't!"

"You black-skinned, back-talking coon, you!" Lee shouted, his face turning crimson with anger.

He struck Christy with the heavy, brass-studded strap. Christy backed out of reach, and when Lee struck him the second time, the Negro caught the strap and held on to it. Lee glared at him at first, and then he tried to jerk it out of his grip.

"Mr. Lee, I haven't done anything except catch a few rabbits and raise a few chickens and things like that," Christy protested. "I didn't mean any harm at all. I thought you'd be pleased if I put some new pickets in your fence."

"Shut your mouth and get that shirt and pants off like I told you," he said, angrier than ever. "And turn that strap loose before I blast it loose from you."

Christy stayed where he was and held on to the strap with all his might. Lee was so angry he could not speak after that. He ran to the closet and got his pistol. He swung around and fired it at Christy three times. Christy released his grip on the strap and sank to the floor.

Lee's brother, Morgan, and the bookkeeper, Hendricks, came running into the back room. [...]

"You and Hendricks heard him threaten to kill me. I had to shoot him down to protect my own life."

They left the back room and went into the front office. Several clerks from the plantation store ran in and wanted to know what all the shooting was about.

"Just a biggity nigger," Lee said, washing his hands at the sink. "He was that Alabama nigger that came over here two or three months ago. I sent for him this morning to ask him what he meant by putting up new pickets in the fence around his house without asking me first. When I got him in here, he threatened me. He was a bad nigger."

From: The Stories of Erskine Caldwell, The University of Georgia Press, Athens, Georgia (USA) 1996, pp. 264ff.

1. Speculate on how the story continues.
   Write an end to the story in which you employ dialogue passages between Christy Tucker and Mr Crossman.
2. Give the complete story a suitable title.
3. Explain your decision to end the story this particular way.
4. Together with a partner, perform the dialogue(s) between Christy Tucker and Mr Crossman.

Kreativität ist bei dieser Aufgabenstellung ausdrücklich erwünscht – je nach Gusto dürfen die Schüler der Geschichte ein positives oder negatives Ende geben. Obwohl das (negative) Ende der Geschichte absehbar und wahrscheinlich ist, tendieren Schüler oft dazu, eher ein Happy End zu gestalten. Wenn sie dies argumentativ begründen, ist dies auch akzeptabel. Im Sinne einer „klassischen" Short Story wäre natürlich auch ein offenes Ende denkbar. Hier kann sich im Anschluss an die Präsentation der Geschichten und Dialoge ein Unterrichtsgespräch anschließen, in dem über das tatsächliche Ende der Geschichte diskutiert wird. Schließlich erhalten die Schüler die zweite Hälfte der Geschichte (und den Titel) und können dann in häuslicher Bearbeitung auf die folgenden Fragen eingehen:

1. Explain why Mr Crossman is so upset.
   Shouldn't he be pleased to have a thorough and hard-working man like Christy?
2. Explain what life is like for the inhabitants of Mr Crossman's plantation. How is the plantation organized?
3. Give examples from the text that show Christy's desperate and hopeless situation. Does he have any chance at all?

Mögliche Antworten:

1.
   - he wants to control Christy and teach him to "stay in his place"
   - he strictly demands the following of his orders and gets furious about independent actions
   - by keeping his (black) sharecroppers in total dependency on his good will, he is in control of everything and can make the most money out of it
   - most likely his intention was not to kill Christy but merely to punish and humiliate him severely; possibly he was taken by surprise by Christy's resistance and the situation got out of control
2.
   - obviously the plantation is organized strictly hierarchically – Mr Crossman as the owner is the boss, followed by white foremen and administration staff – most likely the black workers and sharecroppers are at the lower/lowest end of the hierarchy and controlled by people working on a higher level
3.
   - there are many hints given in the text that show that Christy didn't have any chance right from the beginning; Mr Crossman asks Christy trick (rhetorical) questions which he can't escape (You're one of these biggity niggers, ain't you?; You ain't a Georgia nigger, are you?; Didn't they teach you ...?; Why don't you ...?; Who told your wife ...?; etc.)
   - the choice of words indicates Christy's hopeless situation: nigger;

keep your black face shut; biggity niggers; we teach them ...; stop arguing with me ...; that's my business ...; etc.

- the roles reverse: whereas Christy talks much more than Mr Crossman at the beginning – he hardly talks at the end and Mr Crossman's comments get longer and longer
- Christy's use of English is rather fluent and he is quite eloquent – in contrast to that, Mr Crossman's English is more colloquial and grammatically inaccurate (ain't; I don't want no ...; you ... coon ...)

2.3 Poetical approaches to lynching

Langston Hughes' Gedicht ***The bitter river* (*Copy 9,* S. 36)** ist als *narrative poem* eine Mischung aus Nachruf anlässlich der Ermordung der beiden schwarzen Jugendlichen und einer politischen Anklage aus der Perspektive der *Civil Rights.* Die Schüler erhalten dazu folgende Hintergrundinformationen:

l. 28, The Scottsboro boys: Nine African American teenagers who, after nearly being lynched, were tried and imprisoned in 1931 for the supposed rape of two white women. The Supreme Court overturned the decision, but the State of Alabama continued to prosecute members of the group.
l. 29, Lewis Jones: British novelist (1897–1939), imprisoned for his involvement in the Communist Party.
l. 32, Jim Crow: Discriminatory laws enforcing racial segregation in the South between 1877 and the 1950s.

Als kreativen Einstieg sollen sich die Schüler auf eine Fantasiereise in die Vergangenheit begeben. Dazu können sie in Gruppen von zwei bis drei Schülern arbeiten:

An ancient river remembers and speaks:
Imagine you are a river running through the *Deep South.* Try to remember and think about what you
a) have seen b) have heard c) have smelled d) have known
about people living along the river, the death of people, historical events, wars, slaves, foremen, Southern Belles, parties, lynchings, people crossing the river, famous people, wonderful animals, beautiful flowers, poverty, towns and cities, etc.

Write a poem about your memories, each of your verses should start like this: *I have seen ... I have smelled ... I have heard ...*
You can also add impressions: *I have seen the beauty of nature ... and then the ugliness of war ... I have smelled ... and then ...*
Don't forget to give your poem a title.

Die Gedichte werden dann im Kurs – zum Beispiel mit verteilten Rollen – vorgetragen. Anschließend erhalten die Schüler ***Copy 9.*** Da das Gedicht sehr viele unterschiedliche Motive und Aspekte in bildlich-metaphorischer Form aufgreift, ist es sinnvoll, diese Fülle zu ordnen und in Form einer Mindmap festzuhalten.

Read the poem *The bitter river* by Langston Hughes and find out which different motives and historical and political aspects and allusions are employed. Make a mind map in which you arrange these topics and motives.

Langston Hughes: The bitter river

Dedicated to the memory of Charlie Lang and Ernest Green, each fourteen years old when lynched together beneath the Shubuta Bridge over the Chicasawhey River in Mississippi, October 12th, 1942

There is a bitter river
Flowing through the South.
Too long has the taste of its water
Been in my mouth.
There is a bitter river
Dark with filth and mud.
Too long has its evil poison
Poisoned my blood.
I've drunk of the bitter river
And its gall coats the red of my tongue,
Mixed with the blood of the lynched boys
From its iron bridge hung,
Mixed with the hopes that are drowned there
In the snake-like hiss of its stream
Where I drank of the bitter river
That strangled my dream:
The book studied – but useless,
Tools handled – but unused,
Knowledge acquired but thrown away,
Ambition battered and bruised.
Oh, water of the bitter river
With your taste of blood and clay,
You reflect no stars by night,
No sun by day.

The bitter river reflects no stars –
It gives back only the glint of steel bars
And dark bitter faces behind the steel bars:
The Scottsboro boys behind steel bars,
Lewis Jones behind steel bars,
The voteless sharecropper behind steel bars,
The labor leader behind steel bars,
The soldier thrown from a Jim Crow bus behind steel bars,
The 15c mugger behind steel bars,
The girl who sells her body behind steel bars,
And my grandfather's back with its ladder of scars,
Long ago, long ago – the whip and the steel bars –
The bitter river reflects no stars.

"Wait, be patient," you say.
"Your folks will have a better day."
But the swirl of the bitter river
Takes your words away.
"Work, education, patience
Will bring a better day."
The swirl of the bitter river
Carries your "patience" away.
"Disrupter! Agitator!
Troublemaker!" you say.
The swirl of the bitter river
Sweeps your lies away.

I did not ask for this river
Nor the taste of its bitter brew.
I was given its water
As a gift from you.
Yours has been the power
To force my back to the wall
And make me drink of the bitter cup
Mixed with blood and gall.

You have lynched my comrades
Where the iron bridge crosses the stream
Underpaid me for my labor,
And spit in the face of my dream.
You forced me to the bitter river
With the hiss of its snake-like song –
Now your words no longer have meaning –
I have drunk at the river too long:
Dreamer of dreams to be broken,
Builder of hopes to be smashed,
Lover from an empty pocket
Of my meagre cash,
Bitter bearer of burdens
And singer of a weary song,
I've drunk at the bitter river
With its filth and its mud too long.
Tired now of the bitter river
Tired now of the pat on the back,
Tired now of the steel bars
Because my face is black,
I'm tired of segregation,
Tired of filth and mud,
I've drunk of the bitter river
And it's turned to steel in my blood.

Oh, tragic bitter river
Where the lynched boys hung,
The gall of your bitter water
Coats my tongue.
The blood of your bitter water
For me gives back no stars.
I'm tired of the bitter river:
Tired of the bars!

1942/43

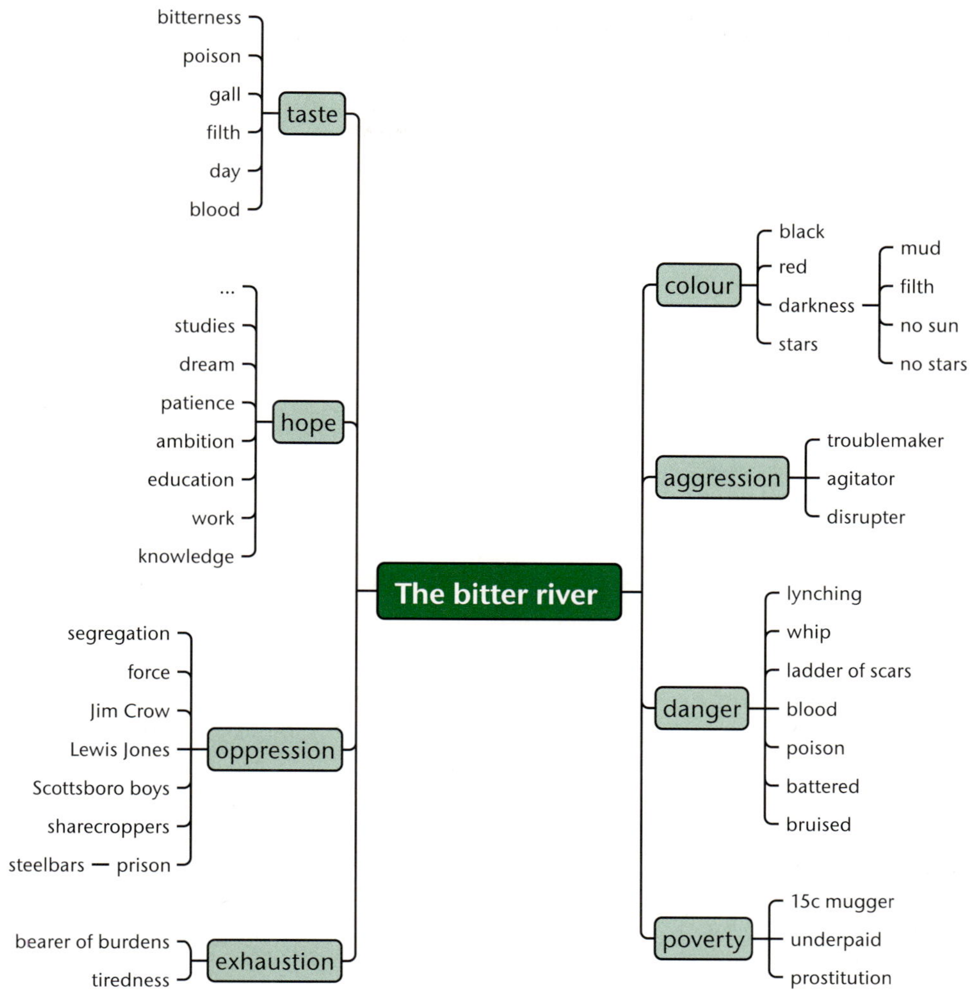

Bei dem Gedicht *The lynching* von Claude McKay, einem Vertreter der *Harlem Renaissance,* aus dem Jahr 1922 **(*Copy 10,* S. 38)** handelt es sich mit 14 Versen um ein klassisches Sonett: Es hat drei Quartette mit jeweils einem umschließenden Reim (abba cddc effe) sowie einem Reimpaar (gg). Damit ist es in der Form den *Shakespearean-style sonnets* zuzuordnen. Auch durch den Satzbau bilden die drei Quartette jeweils eine Einheit. Während die erste Strophe den zum himmlischen Vater aufsteigenden Geist des Gelynchten beschreibt, thematisiert die zweite Strophe den in der Nacht über dem toten Körper wachenden Stern. Im Kontrast zu den eher mitleidsvollen Tönen der ersten beiden Strophen beschreibt die dritte Strophe die Gefühlskälte der Weißen, die bei Tagesanbruch beim grausigen Anblick des Leichnams keine Trauer empfinden. Das Gedicht schließt mit dem Paarreim, der in einer Klimax darstellt, wie Kinder (zukünftige Lyncher) um den Leichnam herumtanzen und dabei teuflische Freude empfinden. Im Vergleich mit dem Gedicht von Langston Hughes mutet es recht altmodisch an, ist aber in seiner Aussage ähnlich hoffnungslos und desillusionierend. Auch aufgrund seiner klaren formalen Strukturierung eignet es sich gut als Hausaufgabe für eine Gedichtanalyse.

Read the poem *The lynching* by Claude McKay and do the tasks on the worksheet (*Copy 10*).

Lösungsvorschlag zu *Copy 10:*

1. *The lynching* is a traditional Shakespearean-style sonnet: it has 14 verses, 3 quatrains with an enclosed rhyme (abba cddc effe) and a couplet (gg) that serves as the climax to the poem. Whereas the first stanza emphasizes religious aspects such as the redemption

Claude McKay: The lynching (1922)

His spirit in smoke ascended to high heaven.
His father, by the cruelest way of pain,
Had bidden him to his bosom once again;
The awful sin remained still unforgiven.
All night a bright and solitary star
(Perchance the one that ever guided him,
Yet gave him up at last to Fate's wild whim)
Hung pitifully o'er the swinging char.
Day dawned, and soon the mixed crowds came to view
The ghastly body swaying in the sun:
The women thronged to look, but never a one
Showed sorrow in her eyes of steely blue;
And little lads, lynchers that were to be,
Danced round the dreadful thing in fiendish glee.

From: James Weldon Johnson (ed.): The Book of American Negro Poetry. New York: Harcourt, Brace and Company, 1922

Lynching of Joseph Richardson, September 26, 1913 in Leitchfield, Kentucky

Lynching of four unidentified African-Americans, ca. 1900

1. Analyse the given sonnet and explain in what way the structural devices match its content.
2. Compared to the song *Strange Fruit* – what are the striking differences and similarities concerning structure, content and the message of the poems in general? In what way do both of the poems depict the horrors of lynching?

of the lynched man, the second stanza reveals that most likely the guiding star did not protect the man while he was still alive, but now pitifully illuminates the darkness of the night. The third stanza describes the emotionless brutality of the white people, and the final couplet foreshadows the gruesome future: even little (white) children don't feel pity – they dance around the corpse of the lynched man hanging in the sun.

2. Both of the poems have a regular structure and a rather traditional rhyme scheme; whereas *The lynching* puts more emphasis on religious aspects such as redemption (for the victim), both poems show a climatic development (burning flesh – children dancing in fiendish glee); similar too is the contrast of the world of the whites and the world of the Blacks respectively describing the contradictory and indifferent behaviour of the whites: pastoral/gallant vs. crime/sadism and women thronged to look vs. steely blue eyes/future lynchers.

2.4 The "cases" Emmett Till and Medgar Evers and reactions of artists

Die Vielschichtigkeit dieser Fälle sowie enorme politische und gesellschaftliche Resonanz, die diese Mordfälle nach sich gezogen haben, lassen es sinnvoll erscheinen, in einer arbeitsteiligen Gruppenarbeit ein *role play* in Form einer Gerichtsverhandlung oder eines Wiederaufnahmeverfahrens der Fälle durchzuführen. Dazu erhalten die Schüler als Einstiegsinformation ***Copy 11*, S. 40** zu einer ersten Orientierung.

1. Read the text about the murder of Emmett Till in 1955 and make a list of the important facts given on that case.
2. Do research on the Internet on the murder of Emmett Till and its aftermath. These websites will help you:
   - www.pbs.org/wgbh/amex/till/
   - www.watson.org/~lisa/blackhistory/early-civilrights/emmett.html
3. Use your notes on the Emmett Till case and prepare a role play that depicts a situation at court. As there is new evidence, the Emmett Till case is about to be reopened at the US Court of Appeals that plans to reinvestigate the lynching. Prepare role cards for the following persons:
   a) the defendants J. W. Milam and Roy Bryant
   b) a lawyer representing the prosecution
   c) a defense counsel
   d) witnesses, e. g. Mose Wright, Emmett's uncle, and Carolyn Bryant
   e) a medical examiner who has examined Emmett's corpse
   Form groups of 5 to 6 students and perform the trial.
   The students watching the performance should later on serve as a jury that has to find a verdict.

The murder of Emmett Till

In August 1955, a fourteen year old boy went to visit his relatives near Money, Mississippi. Intelligent and bold, with a slight mischievous streak, Emmett Till had experienced segregation in his hometown of Chicago, but he was unaccustomed to the severe segregation he encountered in Mississippi. When he showed some local boys a picture of a white girl who was one of his friends back home and bragged that she was his girlfriend, one of them said, "Hey, there's a [white] girl in that store there. I bet you won't go in there and talk to her." Emmett want in and bought some candy. As he left, he said "Bye baby" to Carolyn Bryant, the wife of the store owner.

Although they were worried at first about the incident, the boys soon forgot about it. A few days later, two men came to the cabin of Mose Wright, Emmett's uncle, in the middle of the night. Roy Bryant, the owner of the store, and J. W. Milam, his brother-in-law, drove off with Emmett. Three days later, Emmett Till's body was found in the Tallahatchie River. One eye was gouged out, and his crushed-in head had a bullet in it. The corpse was nearly unrecognizable; Mose Wright could only positively identify the body as Emmett's because it was wearing an initialed ring.

At first, local whites as well as Blacks were horrified by the crime. Bryant and Milam were arrested for kidnapping even before Emmett's body was found, and no local white lawyers would take their case. Newspapers and white officials reported that all "decent" people were disgusted with the murder and proclaimed that "justice would be done."

The Emmett case quickly attracted national attention. Mamie Bradley, Emmett's mother, asked that the body be shipped back to Chicago. When it arrived, she inspected it carefully to ensure that it really was her son. Then, she insisted on an open-casket funeral, so that "all the world [could] see what they did to my son." Over four days, thousands of people saw Emmett's body. Many more Blacks across the country who might not have otherwise heard of the case were shocked by pictures of the corpse that appeared in *Jet* magazine. These pictures moved Blacks in a way that nothing else had. [...]

Whites in Mississippi resented the Northern criticism of the "barbary of segregation" and the NAACP's labelling of the murder as a lynching. Five prominent lawyers stepped forward to defend Milam and Bryant, and officials who had at first denounced the murder began supporting the accused murderers. The two men went on trial in a segregated courthouse in Sumner, Mississippi on September 19, 1955.

The prosecution had trouble finding witnesses to testify against the two men. At that time in Mississippi, it was unheard of for a Black to publicly accuse a white of committing a crime. Finally, Emmett's sixty-four year old uncle Mose Wright stepped forward. When asked if he could point out the two men who had taken his nephew that dark summer night, he stood, pointed to Milam and Bryant, and said "Dar he" – "There he is." Wright's bravery encouraged other Blacks to testify against the two defendants.

In the end, however, even the incredible courage of these Blacks did not make a difference. Defense attorney John C. Whitten told the jurors in his closing statement, "Your fathers will turn over in their graves if [Milam and Bryant are found guilty] and I'm sure that every last Anglo-Saxon one of you has the courage to free these men in the face of that [outside] pressure." The jurors listened to him. They deliberated for just over an hour, then returned a "not guilty" verdict on September 23rd, the 166th anniversary of the signing of the Bill of Rights.

www.watson.org/~lisa/blackhistory/early-civilrights/emmett.html [01.04.2008]

Der Lynchmord an Emmett Till und die damit verbundene öffentliche Diskussion inspirierte Bob Dylan zu seinem Protestlied, das zur Zeit der Studentenunruhen und der Bürgerrechtsbewegung in den USA und darüber hinaus großen Bekanntheitsgrad erlangte. Nur gut ein Jahr später, 1963, schrieb die afro-amerikanische Sängerin **Nina Simone** ihren berühmten Song ***Mississippi Goddam,*** mit dem sie sich auch auf aktuelle politische Ereignisse bezog: die Ermordung des NAACP-Führers Medgar Evers (Juni 1963) und die Bombardierung der *16th Street Baptist Church* in Birmingham, Alabama, durch den Ku Klux Klan, bei der vier 11- bis 14-jährige Kinder getötet und zahlreiche Kirchenbesucher verletzt wurden.

Hierzu informieren sich die Schüler vorbereitend im Internet, z. B. auf den Websites: www.historylearningsite.co.uk/medgar_evers.htm sowie über das Attentat in Birmingham: www.english.uiuc.edu/maps/m_r/randall/birmingham.htm. In arbeitsteiliger Gruppenarbeit in Gruppen zu je 4 bis 5 Schülern untersuchen die Schüler die Songtexte (***Copy 12,* S. 42** und ***Copy 13,* S. 43**) auf ihren Inhalt und ihre Aussage hin und setzen ihre Ergebnisse in Bezug zu dem tatsächlichen Mordfall Emmett Till sowie der Ermordung Medgar Evers und dem Birmingham-Attentat. Dafür sollte man ca. 30 Minuten einplanen.

In einem zweiten Schritt werden die Gruppen gemixt und informieren sich jeweils gegenseitig über ihren Text und ihre Ergebnisse. Daran anschließen sollte sich ein Gespräch im Plenum. Als Hilfestellung für die Textanalyse können die Schüler wiederum ***Copy 17,* S. 52** einsetzen.

Die **CD** zum Unterrichtsmodell stellt den Dylan-Song auf Track 5 zur Verfügung, sodass die Schüler auch einen musikalischen Eindruck bekommen. Man kann den Song als „typisches" Protestlied dieser Zeit bezeichnen: Bob Dylan begleitet seinen Gesang auf der Gitarre, die Melodie weist keine Besonderheiten auf, der Schwerpunkt liegt eindeutig auf dem Inhalt des Textes. Der Song *Mississippi Goddam'*, gesungen von der Jazzsängerin Nina Simone, kann auch bei YouTube angehört bzw. angesehen werden: www.youtube.com/watch?v=ckarOiWLLtY

Form groups of 4 to 5 students and examine the content of the songs.

a) In what way do the lyrics bear reference to
- the murder of Emmett Till,
- the life and death of Medgar Evers and the Birmingham church bombing?

b) Evaluate the songs, stating to what extent they artistically address the smouldering problem of racism, racial inequality and social unrest.

c) After finishing work in your group, interchange your groups and inform each other about your findings and results.

Zur abschließenden Absicherung werden die Ergebnisse der Gruppenarbeit an der Tafel festgehalten.

Bob Dylan: The death of Emmett Till

Emmett Till

'Twas down in Mississippi not so long ago,
When a young boy from Chicago town stepped through a Southern door.
This boy's dreadful tragedy I can still remember well,
The color of his skin was black and his name was Emmett Till.

Some men they dragged him to a barn and there they beat him up.
They say they had a reason, but I can't remember what.
They tortured him and did some evil things too evil to repeat.
There was screaming sounds inside the barn, there was laughing sounds out on the street.

Then they rolled his body down a gulf amidst a bloody red rain
And they threw him in the waters wide to cease his screaming pain.
The reason that they killed him there, and I'm sure it ain't no lie,
Was just for the fun of killin' him and to watch him slowly die.

And then to stop the United States of yelling for a trial,
Two brothers they confessed that they had killed Emmett Till.
But on the jury there were men who helped the brothers commit this awful crime,
And so this trial was a mockery, but nobody seemed to mind.

I saw the morning papers but I could not bear to see
The smiling brothers walkin' down the courthouse stairs.
For the jury found them innocent and the brothers they went free,
While Emmett's body floats the foam of a Jim Crow southern sea.

If you can't speak out against this kind of thing, a crime that's so unjust,
Your eyes are filled with dead man's dirt, your mind is filled with dust.
Your arms and legs they must be in shackles and chains, and your blood it must refuse to flow,
For you let this human race fall down so God-awful low!

This song is just a reminder to remind your fellow man
That this kind of thing still lives today in that ghost-robed Ku Klux Klan.
But if all of us folks that thinks alike, if we gave all we could give,
We could make this great land of ours a greater place to live.

1. Explain the historical and political background to the metaphor in line 2: "a young boy from Chicago town stepped through a Southern door."
2. In groups, compile a "morning paper" (l. 17) front page that reports on the murder of Emmett Till and the trial:
   a) a front page of the *Mississippi Gazette,*
   b) a front page of *The Chicago Enquirer,*
   c) a front page of a European newspaper like *The Times* or *The Guardian.*

Nina Simone: Mississippi Goddam

The name of this tune is
Mississippi goddam
And I mean every word of
it

Alabamas gotten me so
upset
Tennessee made me lose
my rest
And everybody knows about mississippi goddam

Alabamas gotten me so upset
Tennessee made me lose my rest
And everybody knows about mississippi

Cant you see it
Cant you see it
Its all in the air
I cant stand the pressure much longer
Somebody say a prayer

Alabamas gotten me so upset
Tennessee made me lose my rest
And everybody knows about mississippi goddam

This is a show tune
But the show hasnt been written for it, yet

Hound dogs on my trail
School children sitting in jail
Black cat cross my path
I think every days gonna be my last

Lord have mercy on this land of mine
We all gonna get it in due time
I dont belong here
I dont belong here
I even stopped believing in prayer

Dont tell me
I tell you
Me and my people just about due
Ive been there so I know
They keep on saying go slow!

But thats just the trouble
Do it slow
Washing the windows
Do it slow
Picking the cotton
Do it slow
Youre just plain rotten
Do it slow
Youre too damn lazy
Do it slow
The thinkings crazy
Do it slow

Where am I going
What am I doing
I dont know
I dont know

Just try to do your very best
Stand up be counted with all the rest
For everybody knows about mississippi goddam

I made you thought I was kiddin didnt we

Picket lines
School boycotts
They try to say it's a communist plot
All I want is equality
For my sister my brother my people and me

Yes you lied to me all these years
You told me to wash and clean my ears
And talk real fine just like a lady
And you stop calling ma sister sadie

Oh but this whole country is full of lies
Youre all gonna die and die like flies
I dont trust you any more
You keep on saying go slow!
Go slow!

But thats just the trouble
Do it slow
Desegregation
Do it slow
Mass participation
Do it slow
Reunification
Do it slow
Do things gradually
Do it slow
But bring more tragedy
Do it slow
Why dont you see it
Why dont you feel it
I dont know
I dont know

You dont have to live next to me
Just give me my equality
Everybody knows about mississippi
Everybody knows about alabama
Everbody knows about mississippi goddam

Thats it!

Note: The misspellings in the song text are stylistic devices and on purpose.

Lösungsvorschlag/Tafelbild zu *Copy 12* und *13:*

Emmett Till	Medgar Evers/Birmingham bombing
• some of the factual information has been left out • the song addresses emotions and appeals to people's sense of justice • the song is not aggressive or provocative but focusses on telling a story • references to "Jim Crow", the Klan, injustice, religious allusions → appeal to people's moral responsibility • the human race is in a shameful condition • conciliatory ending: hope for a better future *if* people were more concerned and socially committed	• no *direct* remark about one of the cases • many examples of social injustice/violence/racism, etc. are given: imprisoned children, police dogs attacking demonstrators, fear of being killed, prayer/religion doesn't help anymore, etc. • expression of a feeling of enormous shame: the whole world connects Alabama/Tennessee/Mississippi with crime, racism, violence • advice to "my people" (→ Afro-Americans) to get counted (→ voting), to boycott schools, stand in picket lines, demonstrate • she expresses her mistrust of white promises and politics: desegregation, mass participation, reunification ... were all empty promises that brought more tragedy to the people • Simone's song is highly appellative, accusatory and disenchanted – obviously she doesn't see any chance for white and black people to live together

Die Internetrecherche zu Medgar Evers bietet den Schülern auch Hintergrundwissen für den Text in **Klausur 1**, einem weiteren Protestlied von Bob Dylan. Im Gegensatz zu dem Song über Emmett Till drückt er dort eher seine Hoffnungslosigkeit aus – diese Haltung entspricht eher der von Nina Simone. Auch hier lassen sich viele Parallelen finden.

2.5 Dealing with the horrors of the past

Der Artikel aus der renommierten Zeitung *The Observer* aus dem Jahre 2005 ***(Copy 14*, S. 45 f.*)*** zeigt, dass in Bezug auf Rassismus, Rassentrennung und die damit verknüpften Verbrechen in den USA noch vieles aufzuarbeiten ist. Obwohl einige der spektakulären Mordfälle und Gerichtsverhandlungen nochmals aufgerollt und einige der (weißen) Täter nachträglich verurteilt wurden, leben nach wie vor in vielen Teilen der USA Schwarze und Weiße in verschiedenen, wenn nicht gar in gegensätzlichen Welten. Den Zweifel daran, dass es sich bei der Entschuldigung des Senats wirklich um mehr als einen Akt der nach außen gezeigten *Political Correctness* handelt, drückt auch der Cartoon (S. 46) aus: die *lynchings* werden dort vom Senat als *inconvenience* betrachtet – im Gegensatz beispielsweise zu Bürgerrechtsgruppen, die im Zusammenhang mit Sklaverei und rassistisch motivierten Morden von „Holocaust" – Völkermord – sprechen. In diesem Zusammenhang gibt es einen weiteren informativen Artikel von der BBC, der sich auch auf mögliche Reparationszahlungen bezieht, er ist auf folgender Website nachzulesen: http://news.bbc.co.uk/1/hi/world/americas/4090732.stm

Der Artikel *America apologizes for the horrors of lynching* gibt einen Überblick über die wiederaufgenommenen Verfahren und lässt einige Zeitzeugen sowie Politiker zu Wort kommen. Er kann auch als Vorbereitungstext für Klausur 2 eingesetzt werden, da Bezüge zwischen den USA und Deutschland hergestellt werden.

America apologizes for the horrors of lynching

Senat admits failing to stop 'holocaust' of public executions

Anna Holmes remembers hearing about the bridge when she was a little girl. It stood near where the Collington and Western branches of the Patuxent river met, less than a quarter of a mile from the Marlboro jail.

"I used to hear them talking about the lynchings," said Holmes, 79, who spent her childhood in the area, Prince George's County, Maryland.

Stephen Williams, a black man accused of man-handling a white woman, was beaten and hanged on the bridge in the early hours of 20 October 1894. A masked mob snatched him from his cell and dragged him away as he pleaded for his life.

"When the Marlboro bridge was reached, the rope was quickly tied to the railing and amid piteous groans Williams was hurled into eternity," the Washington Post reported.

There was no federal law against lynching and most states refused to prosecute whites for killing black people. The House of Representatives three times agreed to make lynching a federal offence. Each time, the measure died in the Senate at the hands of southern members.

Tomorrow, too late for Williams and 4,742 others murdered by lynch mobs between 1882 and 1968, the Senate will vote on a motion apologizing for the failure to enact an anti-lynching law first proposed 105 years ago.

'The apology is long overdue,' said Republican Senator George Allen, sponsoring the resolution with Democrat Mary Landrieu.

The action comes amid a flurry of reopenings of civil rights era cases. According to the Southern Poverty Law Centre in Alabama, 25 of them have been re-examined or are under re-examination. This has led to 26 arrests, 21 convictions, two acquittals and a mistrial.

Tomorrow, Edgar Ray Killen will go on trial for the murder of three young civil rights workers, the case that formed the basis for the film *Mississippi Burning*.

This month the body of 14-year-old Emmett Till was exhumed as part of an attempt to prosecute the handful of men still alive who may have been involved in his murder in Mississippi in 1955.

Till's death was a hugely galvanising event for the Civil Rights Movement. Just three months after his death, when Rosa Parks famously refused to give up her seat on an Alabama bus, sparking the bus boycott that would kick-start the civil rights era, Emmett was on her mind.

In 1955, Roy Bryant and his half-brother, J.W. Milam, admitted in a magazine article they had killed Emmett – his 'crime' was to whistle at Roy's wife Carolyn in a drugstore. Their confession came two months after both men had been acquitted by an all-white, male jury who took 67 minutes to return the verdict.

Landrieu and other senators decided to back the bill after seeing the book *Without Sanctuary: Lynching Photography in America*, a collection of postcards taken at lynchings.

Towns across America bear reminders of the shameful tradition. In Alexandria, a lamp-post served to lynch Joseph McCoy on 23 April, 1897. In Annapolis, a bluff near College Creek was the site of Henry Davis's lynching just before Christmas in 1906.

Many African-American families can name an ancestor or friend who fell to mob justice. Fred Tutman of Upper Marlboro can point to a tree on his family's land that a previous owner used for lynching.

'The memories are less vivid for me because of my generation,' said Tutman, 47. 'They are more vivid for my mother and grandmother, who had all kinds of violence perpetrated on them.'

Lynching touched all races and religions. Immigrants were frequent targets, so much that at the start of the 20th century the State Department paid nearly $ 500,000 to China, Italy and Mexico on behalf of lynching victims.

But the killings were mainly in the South and four out of five victims were black, according to statistics compiled by Tuskegee University in Alabama. Many had not been accused of anything more than answering back a white man or looking at a white woman. Black landowners were frequent targets.

Before they were shot or hanged, some victims had their eyes gouged out or their teeth pulled out with pliers, were beaten, burned at the stake, dismembered or castrated.

'It was truly the American holocaust,' said Mark Planning, counsel for the Committee for a Formal Apology. 'There are perceptions that lynchings were carried out on some poor souls who were dragged into the woods. But these were public spectacles.'

Mob killings were often carnival-like events. Refreshments were sold, trains made special trips to lynching sites, schools and businesses closed to let people attend. Newspapers ran adverts for them. Corpses were displayed for days. Victims' ears, fingers and toes became souvenirs.

'Lynching was the socially acceptable way to demonstrate control,' said Lawrence Guyot, 66, a civil rights activist. 'It sent a message that not only did this happen to this person, but if you as a black person thought about stepping outside our racial code, it can happen to you. We want everybody to see it. We want the body to stay up as long as possible and all the gory details to be known.' Seven Presidents argued for making it a federal offence. None of this swayed the Senate, where southerners insisted a federal law would intrude on states' rights.

The current effort was born out of a broader movement to ask Congress to acknowledge wrongs toward African-Americans, including slavery. Support finally arrived for campaigners when the Committee for a Formal Apology sent copies of *Without Sanctuary* to senators.

One postcard, depicting a corpse in 1910, read: 'This is a token of a great day we had in Dallas 3 March.' Another, showing the burnt corpse of William Stanley in Temple, Texas, in 1915, read: 'This is the barbecue we had last night ... your son Joe.'

Avis Thomas Lester, Mark Townsend: America Apologizes for the Horrors of Lynching, in: The Observer, June 12, 2005;

1. Explain what *exactly* the Senate has decided to apologize for.
2. What have been the reactions to the Senate's apology?
3. Why hasn't there been any apology in the past?
4. Do you think that apologizing in this way is appropriate? – What else could have been said or done in order to make up for the crimes?
5. Write a "letter to the editor" in which you react to the article and state your opinion on the lynchings and the Senate's apology.

Lösungsvorschlag:

1. The Senate did not apologize for the crimes committed mostly to African-American people, but for not having been able to put a bill through the Senate that would have made lynching a federal crime – thus leaving jurisdiction to the states themselves – and leaving the victims at the mercy of the local courts and judges.
2. Obviously, the apology was a reaction to the re-opening of several civil rights cases – therefore, it might be considered half-hearted. One senator thought the apology had been long overdue. Recently, there seems to have been greater public interest in the topic: a book about lynching photography has been published and an exhibition has been organized.
3. One civil rights activist explains that lynching has been socially acceptable over a long period of time; racial codes still exist – and people should know about it. Only when confronted with the shameful past was Congress finally willing to acknowledge wrongs.
4. Various answers. The students might argue that paying reparations of course cannot undo the horrors of the past – but, in economically tense times, it might help some (underprivileged) people.
5. Various answers are possible. However, the students should write a formal letter and therefore employ certain phrases (→ use their dictionary).

Component 3

Political protest songs in the tradition of the Civil Rights Movement

Component 3 gibt einen kurzen Einblick in die Geschichte der politisch motivierten Protestlieder und schließt damit den Kreis, der mit *Strange Fruit* als einem der frühen *protest songs* eröffnet wurde. Im Rahmen des hier thematisierten historischen Bezuges des *Civil Rights Movement* sollen schlagwortartig einige zentrale Begriffe geklärt werden. Eine erschöpfende Bearbeitung würde den Rahmen dieses Themenheftes sprengen. Jedoch können politische Protestlieder von Schülern nur verstanden werden, zumal in der historischen Distanz von bis zu achtzig Jahren, wenn ein Mindestmaß an Kenntnis historischer Fakten und Bezüge hergestellt wird. Die Songtexte in diesem *Component* umspannen einen Zeitrahmen, der von 1929 (Louis Armstrong) bis zum Jahr 1991 (Public Enemy) reicht.

3.1 Looking at history

***Copy 15*, S. 49** kann, auf OHP-Folie kopiert, zunächst als Impuls für ein *Brainstorming* genutzt werden. Die Schüler können die Bilder sowie die schlagwortartig eingesetzten Begriffe rund um das Thema nutzen, um Kenntnisse aus dem Englisch- oder Geschichtsunterricht zu reaktivieren.

Als Kopie an die Schüler verteilt, kann die *Copy* auch für eine Recherchehausaufgabe genutzt werden, bei der die entsprechenden Begriffe (möglicherweise arbeitsteilig) recherchiert und durch Fakten ergänzt werden. Die Anzahl der Begriffe kann – je nach Anzahl der Kursteilnehmer und Ausrichtung des Kursthemas – beliebig erweitert werden. Man könnte beispielsweise jedem Schüler des Kurses einen Begriff zuweisen (oder einen Begriff auswählen lassen), den er dann recherchiert und auf einer oder zwei Seiten erläutert und illustriert und in der Folgestunde im Kurs präsentiert. Aus diesen Seiten lässt sich dann eine Wandzeitung, zum Beispiel in Form einer *Timeline,* zum Thema *Civil Rights Movement* erstellen.

Reactivate your knowledge about the history of the Civil Rights Movement in the USA.

a) Do research on the given keywords, and find out more about the origins and the social and political impact of this movement. (Use your history books, your English books, or the Internet.)

b) Compile an information sheet that covers all the necessary details.

c) Together with your fellow students, design a wallpaper timeline of the Civil Rights Movement and display it in your classroom.

Viele der Begriffe bzw. Themen eignen sich auch für umfassendere Projektthemen oder sogar für Facharbeiten; sie können auch im Zusammenhang mit dem Zentralabitur-Schwerpunktthema *The American Dream* bearbeitet werden.

The Civil Rights Movement – a project approach

NAACP

Jim Crow Laws

Malcolm X

Sixteenth Church Birmingham

Selma

Memphis

Black Power

Rosa Parks

FREEDOM SUMMER MISSISSIPPI

CIVIL RIGHTS ACT

EMANCIPATION PROCLAMATION

March on Washington

James Meredith

LITTLE ROCK HIGH SCHOOL

KKK

Black Codes

Brown v. Board of Education

Segregation

Martin Luther King

3.2 The Civil Rights Movement reflected in (protest) songs

Die auf ***Copy 16*, S. 51**, zusammengestellten Songtexte gehören mit zu den bekanntesten „Hymnen" der 1960er- und 1970er-Jahre. Der Song *We shall overcome* ist von unzähligen Künstlern gesungen worden, wurde aber ursprünglich von Pete Seeger aus einem Gospelsong entwickelt. Bei YouTube kann er, diesmal gesungen von Joan Baez, auf folgender Website angehört bzw. angesehen werden: www.youtube.com/watch?v=RkNsEH1GD7Q (4:24 Min.)
Während der Song *Southern man* von Neil Young eine eher melancholisch-ausweglose Perspektive hat, kann man in *To be young, gifted and black* von Nina Simone bereits die Entschlossenheit und Kraft der *black power*- und *black consciousness*-Bewegung spüren, obwohl beide aus dem gleichen Jahr, 1970, stammen. Der Nina-Simone-Song *To be young, gifted and black* kann bei YouTube angehört bzw. angesehen werden: www.youtube.com/watch?v=XD2oJDGfOuk (3:10 Min.)

1. Watch the YouTube video clips showing Joan Baez and Nina Simone and listen to their songs.
   Use *Copy 17* to evaluate and analyse the lyrics and the instrumentation.
2. Read the song text *Southern man* sung by Neil Young and evaluate it.
3. Compare the songs and discuss your findings in class.

Die Songtexte eignen sich gut, um sie auf die heutige Zeit zu beziehen und sie von den Schülerinnen und Schülern auf heutige Probleme und Themen beziehen und umtexten zu lassen. Heute politisch aktuelle Themenbereiche wie Asylpolitik in Deutschland/Europa, Neonazis, Migranten, (Kinder-)Armut, zunehmende soziale Spannungen, Gewalt, usw. können auf diese Weise thematisiert und kreativ verarbeitet werden. Dies bietet auch eine gute Gelegenheit für Wortschatzarbeit zu den o.g. Themen. Alternativ kann man die Schüler auch die Texte mit anderer Musik, z. B. Rap, unterlegen lassen.

Think of current problems and issues like (political) refugees in Germany/Europe, neo-Nazis, migrants, (child) poverty, growing social tensions, violence, AIDS, etc.
Form groups of four students each and write new texts based on the given civil rights protest songs. If you want, you can also use different music.

3.3 Segregation and racism reflected in songs

Der Louis-Armstrong-Song *What did I do to be so black and blue?* **(*Copy 18*, S. 54)**, zur Zeit der Roaring Twenties geschrieben, zeigt, dass selbst ein sehr berühmter afro-amerikanischer Musiker wie Louis Armstrong unter Rassismus und Rassentrennung litt. Obwohl Louis Armstrong schon sehr früh ein Star wurde und sich äußerster Beliebtheit auch bei einem großen weißen Publikum erfreute, galten für ihn die Regeln der Rassentrennung – wie der unten stehende Text belegt. Die außergewöhnliche Persönlichkeit und Karriere von Louis Armstrong eignen sich, ähnlich wie Josephine Baker, sehr gut für ein (größeres) Projekt oder gar eine Facharbeit.

Hymns of the civil rights era

Southern man

Southern man, better keep your head
Don't forget what your good book said
Southern change gonna come at last
Now your crosses are burning fast
Southern man.

I saw cotton and I saw black
Tall white mansions and little shacks.
Southern man, when will you pay them back?
I heard screamin' and bullwhips cracking
How long? How long?

Southern man, better keep your head
Don't forget what your good book said
Southern change gonna come at last
Now your crosses are burning fast
Southern man.

Lily Belle, your hair is golden brown
I've seen your black man comin' round
Swear by God I'm gonna cut him down!
I heard screamin' and bullwhips cracking
How long? How long?

Neil Young, 1970

To be young, gifted and black

To be young, gifted and black,
Oh what a lovely precious dream
To be young, gifted and black
Open your heart to what I mean

In the whole world you know
There are billion boys and girls
Who are young, gifted and black,
And that's a fact!

Young, gifted and black
We must begin to tell our young
There's a world waiting for you
This is a quest that's just begun

When you feel really low
Yeah, there's a great truth you should know
When you're young, gifted and black
You're soul's intact

Young, gifted and black
How I long to know the truth
There are times when I look back
And I am haunted by my youth

Oh but my joy of today
Is that we can all be proud to say
To be young, gifted and black
Is where it's at

Nina Simone, 1970

We shall overcome

We shall overcome, some day.
Oh, deep in my heart,
I do believe
We shall overcome, some day.
We'll walk hand in hand,
We'll walk hand in hand,
We'll walk hand in hand, some day.
Oh, deep in my heart,
We shall live in peace,
We shall live in peace,
We shall live in peace, some day.
Oh, deep in my heart,
We shall all be free,
We shall all be free,
We shall all be free, some day.
Oh, deep in my heart,
We are not afraid,
We are not afraid,
We are not afraid, TODAY
Oh, deep in my heart,
We shall overcome,
We shall overcome,
We shall overcome, some day.
Oh, deep in my heart,
I do believe
We shall overcome, some day.

We Shall Overcome, 1963, Musik/Text: Zilphia Horton/
Frank Hamilton/Pete Seeger/Guy Carawan;

Discourse analysis of (political) songs

How would you characterize and evaluate this song?
Circle the number of your choice: 1 = not at all; 6 = very much

warm	1 2 3 4 5 6	rnakes me want to dance	1 2 3 4 5 6
gentle	1 2 3 4 5 6	inspiring	1 2 3 4 5 6
coarse	1 2 3 4 5 6	soothing	1 2 3 4 5 6
lively	1 2 3 4 5 6	lyrics and music match	1 2 3 4 5 6
soft	1 2 3 4 5 6	I want to hear it again	1 2 3 4 5 6
boring	1 2 3 4 5 6	I would give it to a friend	1 2 3 4 5 6
simple	1 2 3 4 5 6	I think the person singing is:	
aggressive	1 2 3 4 5 6	sincere	1 2 3 4 5 6
fun	1 2 3 4 5 6	in love	1 2 3 4 5 6
shocking	1 2 3 4 5 6	excited	1 2 3 4 5 6
appalling	1 2 3 4 5 6	convincing	1 2 3 4 5 6
accusatory	1 2 3 4 5 6	angry	1 2 3 4 5 6
cynical	1 2 3 4 5 6	bored	1 2 3 4 5 6
good vocals	1 2 3 4 5 6	boring	1 2 3 4 5 6
repetitive	1 2 3 4 5 6	courageous	1 2 3 4 5 6
good beat	1 2 3 4 5 6	frightened	1 2 3 4 5 6
good instrumentation	1 2 3 4 5 6	I would like to meet the singer:	1 2 3 4 5 6
good lyrics	1 2 3 4 5 6	Further comments:	
socio-political	1 2 3 4 5 6		
disorganized	1 2 3 4 5 6	______________________________	
too long	1 2 3 4 5 6	______________________________	
too slow	1 2 3 4 5 6		
registers of English:		______________________________	
poetic	1 2 3 4 5 6		
colloquial	1 2 3 4 5 6	______________________________	
archaic	1 2 3 4 5 6	______________________________	
slang/non-standard English	1 2 3 4 5 6		

What would you like to change about the song?
Write your evaluation of the song in full on the back of this sheet.

✂ -

Often song lyrics express social and cultural values, such as loyalty, independence, etc. Look at the questions below as you listen to the song. Discuss your ideas with your group.

1. What is the main theme or message of the song?
2. Which words tell you the main theme or message?
3. What social or cultural values or issues are reflected in the song?
4. What kinds of people have these values?
5. Which of these values do you agree with?
6. Which of these values do you disagree with?
7. Do you think any of the values/ideas of the song are universal, or are they specific to the country or culture represented by the song?
8. How would the values, images and symbols employed in the song be interpreted in your own culture (e.g. national pride, racism, etc.)?

Louis [Armstrong] was extraordinarily warm-hearted, off the stage as well as on. He was without prejudices of any kind. As a poor boy, he worked for and was nurtured by a Jewish family in New Orleans, and he was fond of Jews for the rest of his life. "I learned a lot from them," he said, "as to how to live – real life and determination." He shared his immeasurable goodwill with all kinds of people; but despite his ever-amiable public image, Louis never forgot what he and other blacks had experienced as objects of bigotry. [...] Photographer Herb Snizter tells of being on the road with Louis in 1960. It was long after he had become world-famous: "We set out on a bright, warm Saturday afternoon, headed north, with everyone in a good mood.

The bus did not have a toilet. So somewhere in Connecticut [not the Deep South], we stopped in order for Louis to go to the bathroom. I was stunned when the owner of the restaurant, clearly on the basis of race, refused him use of otherwise available facilities. I will never forget the look of Louis' face. Here he was, a favorite to millions of people, America's single most identifiable entertainer, and yet excluded in the most humiliating fashion from a common convenience."

http://gadflyonline.com/archive/MarchApril100/archive-louisarmstrong.html [10.08.2008]

1. Find out more about Louis Armstrong's life and career and present your findings to the course/class.
2. Do the tasks on *Copy 18,* and work creatively with the song and the photograph.

Lösungsvorschlag zu *Copy 18:*

a) the song:
   3. This line might have a double meaning: on the one hand, it refers to the fact that inwardly all human beings are the same – and equal. On the other hand, this might be an allusion to Louis Armstrong being called "a white nigger" by some of his critics who thought that he was too subordinate and kind.

b) the picture:
   1. a street in a city; three young African-Americans are standing together, leaning on a mailbox; they look bored and obviously want to appear "cool" and "easygoing"; they seem to be intractable and unruly

Die Songtexte auf ***Copy 19*, S. 55** greifen den Aspekt der Hautfarbe erneut auf, zeigen allerdings auch die Entwicklung des Selbstverständnisses der Schwarzen auf. Von einer eher fatalistischen Haltung *(Trouble* → Blues) über eine Trotzhaltung *(Say it loud ...* → Funk) bis hin zur völligen Ablehnung und provokativen Anti-Haltung, die sich auch sprachlich ausdrückt *(I don' wanna be yo' nigga* → Rap) lässt sich hier sehr deutlich auch die politisch-kulturelle Entwicklung erkennen. Die drei Texte eignen sich daher gut, um an ihnen historische, politische und kulturelle Veränderungen und Trends nachzuvollziehen. Dies kann beispielsweise in arbeitsteiliger Gruppenarbeit in Zusammenhang mit *Copy 15* und dem Erstellen einer *Timeline* erfolgen, der die Schüler bestimmte Songs oder Zeilen aus Songtexten zuordnen. Der James-Brown-Song kann auf folgender Website angesehen bzw. angehört werden: www.youtube.com/watch?v=hKCsUWx-QoA.

Louis Armstrong: What did I do to be so black and blue?

Cold empty bed ... springs hard as lead
Feels like ole Ned ... wished I was dead
What did I do ... to be so black and blue?

Even the mouse ... ran from my house
They laugh at you ... and scorn you too
What did I do ... to be so black and blue?
I'm white ... inside ... but that don't help my case

That's life ... can't hide ... what is in my face
How will it end ... ain't got a friend
My only sin ... is in my skin
What did I do ... to be so black and blue?

I'm white ... inside ... but that don't help my case
Cause I can't hide ... what is in my face
How will it end?

Louis Armstrong, 1929

New York City, ca. 1942, Helen Levitt

a) The song:

1. Make an acrostic with the words "black and blue", and write down what you associate with it.
2. Make imperative sentences beginning with the letters of the word "RACISM", as in an acrostic.
3. Explain the speaker's statement "I'm white ... inside" – what does it express?

b) The picture:

1. Describe the situation – imagine the men's feelings and thoughts.
2. What is about to happen next?
3. Write a story about this picture of a street scene.

Songs about segregation and racism in the course of time

Trouble

Well, I always been in trouble, 'cause I'm a black-skinned man.
Said I hit a white man, [and they] locked me in the can
They took me to the stockade, wouldn't give me no trial
The judge said, "You black boy, forty years on the hard rock pile."

Trouble, trouble, sure you won't make me stay,
Trouble, trouble, jail break due someday.

Wearin' cold iron shackles from my head to my knee
And that mean old keeper, he's all time kickin' me.
I went up to the walker and the head boss too
Said, "You big white folks, please see what you can do."
Sheriff winked at the policeman, said, "I won't forget you nohow,
You better come back and see me again, boy, about forty years from now."
Went back to the walker, he looked at me and said,
"Don't you worry about 40, 'cause in five years you'll be dead."

Trouble, trouble, makes me weep and moan
Trouble, trouble, every since I was born.
Trouble, trouble, sure won't make me stay,
Trouble, trouble, jail break due someday.

Josh White, 1958

Say it loud (I'm black and I'm proud)

Say it loud: I'm black and I'm proud!
Say it loud: I'm black and I'm proud!

Some people say we've got a lot of malice
Some say it's a lot of nerve
But I say we won't quit moving until we get what we deserve
We have been bucked and we have been scorned
We have been treated bad, talked about as just bones
But just as it takes two eyes to make a pair, ha
Brother we can't quit until we get your share

Say it loud: I'm black and I'm proud! (3x)

I worked on jobs with my feet and my hand
But all the work I did was for the other man
Now we demand a chance to do things for ourselves
We're tired of beatin' our head against the wall
And workin' for someone else
Say it loud: I'm black and I'm proud (4x)

We're people, we're just like the birds and the bees,
We'd rather die on our feet
Than be livin' on our knees

Say it loud: I'm black and I'm proud (4x)

I don't wanna be called yo nigga

Yo! Ho! ... yo nigga! yo nigga! no nigga!
Check it out
How can you say to me yo my nigga
Cursin' up a storm with your finger on a trigger
Feelin' all the girls like a big gold digger
Take a small problem
Make a small problem bigger
Yo ain't poor I got dough
Don't consider me your brother no more
Goddam kilogram, how do you figure
I don't want to be called yo nigga
Yo nigga ...
Hey
Yo nigga
I try to make my statements
Stick like a flypaper
Judge says to me yo nigga sign these goddamm papers
My boss told me yo nigga you're fired
Yo nigga this,
Yo nigga that
I know you're a nigga now 'cause your head got fat
Flava framalama boy you won't figure
I don't wanna be called yo nigga
Yo nigga ...
Break it down
N.I.G.G.E.R.
Nigga ...
Everybody sayin' it
Everybody playin' it rolling on the scales
'Cause everybody is weighin' it
Toby say yo I be a good nigga
Let me get a shovel make a good digger
I don't care how small or bigger
I don't want to be called yo nigga
Yo nigga ...

Public Enemy, 1991

Weiterführende Materialien

Filme

- *Strange Fruit,* Joel Katz, California Newsreel 2002, 57 min.
- *Mississippi Burning,* Alan Parker, USA 1988, 122 min.

Sachbücher

- Archer, Jules: *They Had A Dream – The Civil Rights Struggle,* Puffin Books, New York 1993
- Aretha, David: *The Murder of Emmett Till,* Morgan Reynolds Publishing, Greensboro, N.C. 2008
- Blank, Carla (ed.): *Rediscovering America,* Three Rivers Press, New York 2003
- Cash, J.W.: *The Mind of the South,* Vintage Books 1991 (reprint of 1947)
- Chafe, William H. et al (eds.): *Remembering Jim Crow – African Americans Tell About Life in the Segregated South,* New Press, New York 2001
- Chalmers, David M.: *Hooded Americanism – The History of the Ku Klux Klan,* F. Watts, New York 1965
- Cooper Jackson, Esther (ed.): *Freedomways Reader,* Westview Press, USA 2000
- Davis, Angela Y.: *Blues Legacies and Black Feminism,* Vintage, New York 1999
- Dunbar, Leslie: *The Shame of Southern Politics – Essays and Speeches,* The University Press of Kentucky 2002
- Gretlung, Jan N.: *Frames of Southern Mind. Reflections on the Stoic, Biracial and Existential South,* Odense University Press, Denmark 1998
- Hailey, Alex: *The Autobiography of Malcolm X – as told to Alex Hailey,* Ballantine Books, New York 1964
- Harper, Michael S./Walton, Anthony: *The Vintage Book of African American Poetry,* Vintage Books, USA 2000
- Howard-Pitney, David: *Martin Luther King Jr., Malcolm X, and the Civil Rights Struggle of the 1950s and 1960s,* Bedford/St. Martin's, New York 2004
- Jackson Jr., John P.: *Social Scientists for Social Justice – Making the Case Against Segregation,* New York University Press 2001
- Lay, Shawn (ed.): *The Invisible Empire in the West,* University of Illinois Press, Chicago 2004
- Lester, Julius: *To Be A Slave,* Scholastic Inc., USA 1968
- Litwack, Leon F.: *Trouble in Mind – Black Southerners in the Age of Jim Crow,* Vintage Books, New York 1998
- Luedtke, Luther S. (ed.): *Making America – The Society and Culture of the United States,* Forum Series, USIA Washington D.C. 1991
- Margolick, David: *Strange Fruit – Billie Holiday, Café Society and an Early Cry for Civil Rights,* Running Press, Philadelphia 2000
- Patterson, T. R.: *Zora Neale Hurston and a History of Southern Life,* Temple University Press, USA 2005
- Raines, Howell: *My Soul Is Rested – The Story of the Civil Rights Movement in the Deep South,* Putnam's Sons, USA 1977
- Roberts, Gene/Klibanoff, Hank: *The Race Beat,* Vintage Books, USA 2006
- Teague, Bob: *The Flip Side of Soul – Letters to my Son*, Quill Book, New York 1989
- Vincent, Theodore G.: *Black Power and the Garvey Movement,* Black Classic Press, Baltimore 1970
- Wade, Wyn Craig: *The Fiery Cross – The Ku Klux Klan in America,* Simon & Schuster Inc., USA 1987
- Wormser, Richard: *The Rise and Fall of Jim Crow,* Grolier Publishing, USA 1999
- Wright, Gavin: *Old South – New South,* Basic Books, USA 1986

Bildbände

- Allen, James et al: *Without Sanctuary – Lynching Photography in America,* Twin Palms Publishers 2007
- Boyd, Herb: We shall overcome, Sourcebooks, Illinois, 2004 (including 2 Audio CDs)
- Lanker, Brian: *I Dream A World – Portraits of Black Women Who Changed America,* Suart, Taboro & Chang, New York 1999
- Marable, M., Mullings L.: *Freedom – A Photographic History of the African-American Struggle,* Phaidon Press, London 2002

Unterrichtsmaterialien

- Carson, Mary Kay: *The Underground Railroad for Kids,* Chicago Review Press 2005
- Field, Ron: *African Peoples of the Americas – From Slavery to Civil Rights,* Cambridge University Press 1995
- Murphy: Tim: *Music and Song,* OUP 1992
- Smith, Nigel: *Black Peoples of the Americas,* OUP 1992
- Spiro, Jane: *Creative Poetry Writing,* OUP 2004

Romane, Short Stories

- Bierce, Ambrose: *An Occurrence At Owl Creek Bridge*
- Caldwell, Erskine: *Saturday Afternoon* (1931)
- Caldwell, Erskine: *The End of Christy Tucker*
- Welty, Eudora: *Where is the Voice Coming from* (on the assassination of Medgar Evers, 1963)

Internetadressen

- www.nationalgeographic.com/railroad (Underground Railroad interaktiv)
- www.bcri.org (Birmingham Civil Rights Institute)
- http://www.kinginstitute.info/ (The Martin Luther King, Jr., Research And Education Institute
- http://sunsite.unc.edu/south/ (The American South: Internet Resource Center)

Zeitschriften, Magazine, Artikel

- Bullard, Sara (ed.): *Free At Last – A History of the Civil Rights Movement,* Teaching Tolerance, Montgomery, Alabama 1997
- Cohen, Roger: *Race and American Memory,* The New York Times, April 17,2008, in: http://www.nytimes.com/2008/04/17/opinion/17cohen.html?_r=1&oref=slogin
- Dickey, Christopher: *Southern Discomfort – The Mind of the American South,* in: Newsweek, August 11, 2008, pp. 36ff.
- Griffin, Nancy/Freeman, Morgan: *Back Home – What lured the actor back to his Mississippi roots,* in: AARP The Magazine, November/December 2007, Cover Story, S. 62–67, 108
- Puckrein, Gary A.: *The Civil Rights Movement and the Legacy of Martin Luther King Jr.,* United States Information Agency, Washington D.C. 1993
- Tomasky, Michael: *Obama victory celebrates civil rights journey that began with freedom rides,* in: The Guardian, Thursday June 5,2008, in: www.guardian.co.uk/commentisfree/2008/jun/05/barackobama.uselections2008

Musik (Auswahl) zu *social criticism, civil rights, the South*

- Brown, James: *The Very Best Of,* Polydor 2002
- Chapman, Tracy: *Tracy Chapman,* Elektra 1988
- Chapman, Tracy: *Crossroads,* Elektra 1989
- Crosby, Stills, Nash & Young: *4 Way Street,* Atlantic 1970
- Crosby, Stills, Nash & Young: *American Dream,* Warner Music Group 1988

- Dylan, Bob: *The Times they are a-Changin',* Sony BMG Music 1964 (remastered 2005)
- Seeger, Pete: *Greatest Hits,* Sony Music 2001
- Simone, Nina: *Hits and Classics,* Ariola 2001
- *The Wonderful Music of Billie Holiday,* Intermusic S.A. 1996
- Young, Neil: *Living With War,* Warner Music Group 2006

CD-Verzeichnis

Track 1: Billie Holiday: Strange Fruit (3:11)
von der CD: The Wonderful Music of Billie Holiday. WMO 90302 (LC 03328, Megaphon Importservice), issued under license to Intermusic S.A., © 1996 Intermusic S.A., ℗ Movieplay S.A.

Track 2: Cassandra Wilson: Strange Fruit (4:58, gekürzt)
von der CD: Cassandra Wilson: New Moon Daughter. CDP 724383718320 (LC 0133, Blue Note Records, registered trademark of Capitol Records), © ℗ 1995 Capitol Records, Inc.

Track 3: Sting and Gil Evans: Strange Fruit (6:25, gekürzt)
von der CD: Sting and Gil Evans: Strange Fruit. ITM 1499 (CODAEX), © ℗ 1997 Records

Track 4: UB40: Strange Fruit (4:06)
von der CD: UB40: Signing Off. CDOVD439 (LC 3098), © ℗ 1980 Virgin Records Ltd.

Track 5: Bob Dylan: The Death of Emmett Till (1:42, gekürzt)
von der CD: Documents of Bob Dylan. CD 31004, LP 11004, Magic Music

Track 6: J. J. Cale, Magnolia (2:33, gekürzt)
von der CD: The Very Best of J. J. Cale. 534754-2 (LC 0268), © 1997 PolyGram International Music B.V.

Bildnachweis

S. 3 o.l., 18, 38: Allen/Littlefield Collection; S. 3 o.r.: taken from „Mississippi Burning", © 1988 Orion Pictures Corporation Inc.; S. 3 u.: © TerraVista/LOOK-foto; S. 17 u.l.: taken from youtube.com; S. 17 u.r.: akg-images/Erich Lessing © The Munch Museum/The Munch Ellingsen Group/VG Bild-Kunst, Bonn 2008; S. 25 o.l.: Abel Meeropol Collection, Department of Special Collections, Boston University; S. 25 o.r.: Photography by Charles Peterson, courtesy of Don Peterson, Jazz Photo Collection; S. 26: Courtesy of The New Yorker, Condé Nast Publications, Inc.; S. 42: Library of Congress; S. 46: © 2005 Khalil Bendib; S. 49 o.l.: © Fred Ward/Black Star; S. 49 o.r.: Corbis; S. 49 u.l.: Chicago Historical Society (ICHI-19483); S. 49 u.r.: Associated Press; S. 54: © Helen Levitt, New York

Sollte trotz aller Bemühungen um korrekte Urheberangaben ein Irrtum unterlaufen sein, bitten wir darum, sich mit dem Verlag in Verbindung zu setzen, damit wir eventuell erforderliche Korrekturen vornehmen können.

EinFach Englisch
Unterrichtsmodelle

Herausgegeben von Hans Kröger

Schöningh Verlag
Postfach 2540
33055 Paderborn

Schöningh

Fordern Sie unseren Prospekt zur kompletten Reihe an:
Informationen 0800 / 18 18 787 (freecall)
info@schoeningh.de / www.schoeningh-schulbuch.de